a collection of deli

GW00580008

herbs and spices

Contents

Text by Sara Burford.
This edition published in 2009 by L&K Designs.
© L&K Designs 2009
PRINTED IN CHINA

Publishers Disclaimer

The recipes contained in this book are passed on in good faith but the publisher cannot be held responsible for any adverse results. Please be aware that certain recipes may contain nuts.

Herbs & Spices – What's the Difference?

The difference between herbs and spices is, in essence, fairly simple; the key to differentiation is in knowing where the plant species originates from and what part of the plant is being utilised.

Plants bearing spices predominantly originate from, and grow in, tropical climates. The spices are derived from the seeds, bark, flowers, rhizomes, buds, fruit or root of plants or trees; e.g. ginger, from roots – cumin, from seeds. Spices are largely more potent in flavour and are usually produced for distribution in dried form, either whole or crushed.

Plants bearing herbs can be grown in varying temperate climates; as well as some being able to grow and thrive, both in, or out doors. Most herbs are taken from the aromatic, green parts of plants or shrubs; i.e. the leaves and tender stem. Herbs are made available in either fresh or dried form – when dried, they can be utilised either crushed or whole.

Another quite significant difference between herbs and spices, is the way in which they are utilised in recipes and technically, how they are best cooked and at what point they are added to the cooking process. For example, herbs are generally used in larger quantities than spices, due to strength of taste of spices.

Herbs and spices have been in human circulation since biblical times – and in some cases, even longer.

Herbs

The vast majority of herbs were initially recognised in ancient civilisations in a much-respected medicinal capacity, only later becoming a welcome addition to cooking. Flavouring and enhancing foods, as well as providing satisfactory nourishment, herbs made even the blandest foods taste more appealing to their experimental chefs. Their remarkable journey, to almost every corner of the globe, has brought culinary-pleasure to even the most cautious and conservative of taste buds.

Interestingly, the pronunciation of the word 'herb', historically, did not annunciate the 'h'. Nowadays, only the Americans give it that original treatment, with many assuming that they have the wrong end of the linguistic-stick!

Spices

Spices have a slightly more controversial and contentious history, recognised for their culinary uses, they were also much sought after commodity for their valuable trading and monetary value; making them the subject and inspiration of explorations and the historically infamous, 'spice trade', which resulted in piracy, deception and merciless dealings between traders - and which ultimately, became a pivotal factor in the rise and fall of some very powerful world empires.

Thankfully, today they are no longer the cause of such debacles and are loved as a popular culinary favourite in kitchens all over the world.

Hints and Tips

Hints and Tips

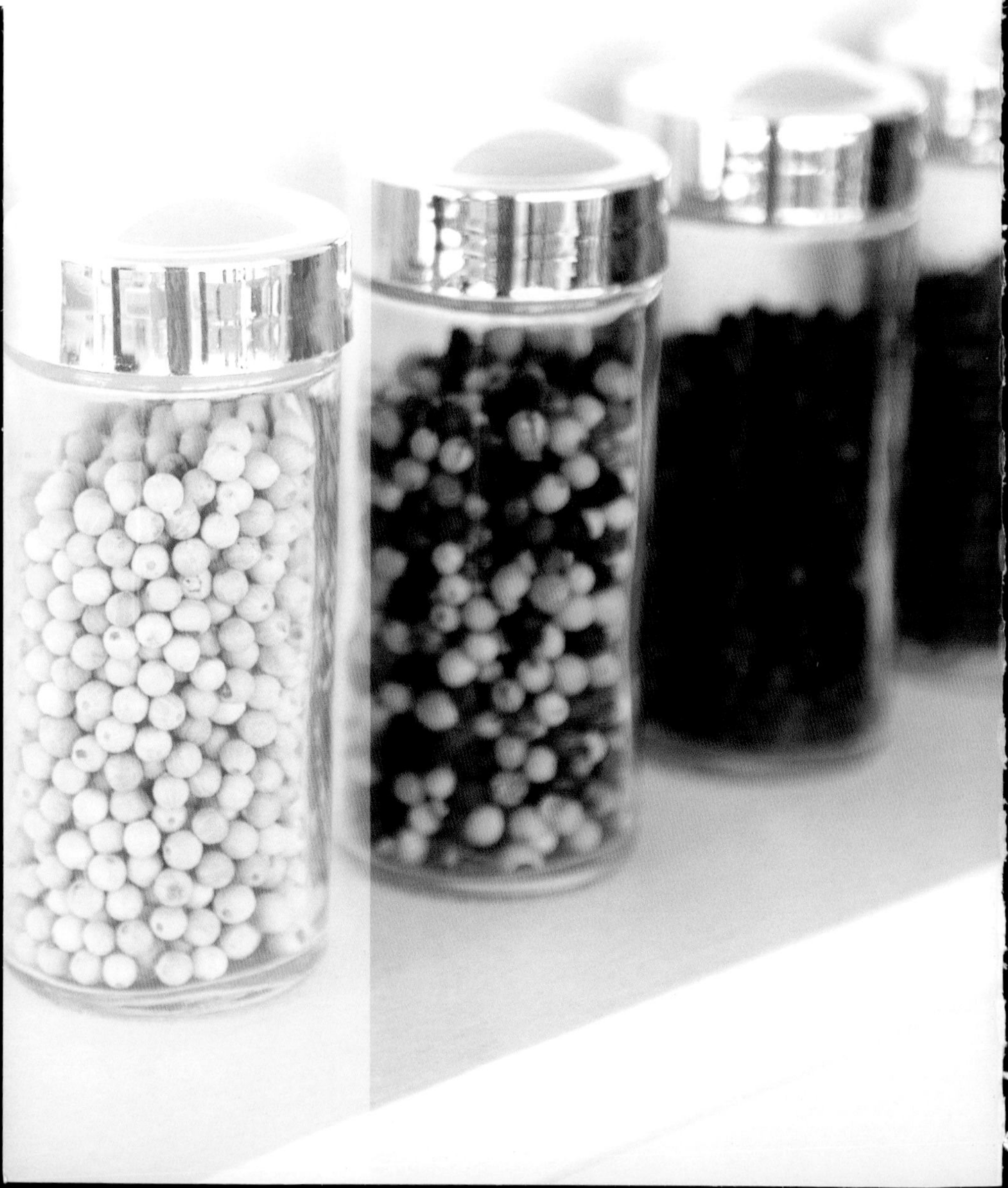

Herb and spice up your life!

Experimenting with recipes using herbs and spices is a fabulous and fun way of bringing world cuisine into your home; livening up your cooking, filling your home with deliciously inviting aromas and giving your taste buds a well-deserved change of scene!

Herbs and spices not only taste great, they're also low-fat and provide a range of health benefits; ranging from aiding digestion and relieving nausea, to relieving the symptoms of respiratory illness and toothache.

The world is your oyster in terms of flexing your own personal likes and dislikes. Flavour your dishes with the specified recipe measure and once you're a little more confident, you can always adjust the amounts, or even the choice of herbs and spices that you use. You might even feel brave enough to make your own unique herb and spice mixes!

Whether you want to use them for baking or cooking, as an alternative flavouring for drinks, or as a garnish or condiment; the vast majority of herbs and spices are largely accessible from most supermarkets and home stores. For those which are a little harder to come by, your local directory should be able to provide details of speciality retailers in your area.

Each region of the world has its own preferred cuisine, typically influenced by the herbs and spices native to that part of the world. Whether it be the exotic and intense spices of India, or the warm and earthy herbs of the Mediterranean; these flavourings inject a delicious variety of tastes, colours, sensations and aromas to their chosen dishes.

If you grew up in the UK, chances are that you may have experienced the post-war leaning towards 'meat and two-veg', with not many varying flavourings and seasonings; and a swift downward turn in home baking. Thankfully, the rise of world-cuisine restaurants in the high streets have provided the opportunity to taste, and appreciate, all the different flavours and ways in which herbs and spices can enrich our food.

This relatively new relationship with Indian, Chinese, Thai, Italian, Greek, Turkish and Middle Eastern cuisine; (to name but a few); has stirred our culinary interest and spurred us on to introduce it into our lives, homes and kitchens.

Hints, Tips & Tools

Be Economical
As crushed and ground herbs lose their flavour and potency much quicker than fresh, it is more economical to buy smaller sized jars or packets, unless you know you're going to use a particular herb or spice enough to exhaust your supplies.

Bulk Buying
Be wary of buying spices from wholesale, bulk retailers, as sometimes old herbs and spices may be mixed with the newer ones. A cheaper bulk price might not mean that you get an honest bargain.

Check for Aroma
When crushing whole spices or herbs, if you don't detect an aroma then they have lost their taste and need to be discarded and replaced.

Dried Herbs
To release natural, essential oils and enrich the flavour of dried herbs, crush them between your palms before adding to recipes.

Dried Herbs Vs Fresh Herbs
When cooking with dried herbs, whilst referring to a recipe using fresh herbs, use only 1/3 of the amount recommended for the fresh herbs, e.g. 1 tablespoon of fresh herbs, should convert to 1 teaspoon of dried herbs. The flavour of dried herbs is more intense, so will overpower a recipe if added at the same measure as fresh herbs.

Add dried herbs near the beginning of cooking, so that the flavour has time to develop. Fresh herbs should be added near to the end of cooking, (unless the recipe specifies otherwise), to preserve the delicate, less intense flavours and aromas.

Dry-Toasting
For a more intense and potent flavour when making spice mix recipes, prior to grinding, dry-toast the whole spices in a frying pan, over a high heat until the aroma is released. Allow to cool before grinding. This process will release more flavour, making it far more pleasurable!

7

Electric Tools

If you don't have an electric spice grinder, a coffee grinder will suffice – although once used for spices, it's advisable not to use again for grinding coffee. It's an idea to invest in one coffee grinder for coffee and one for spices.

Improvise!

Improvise if you don't have any of the 'correct' equipment for crushing spices; place the whole spices between two clean cloths and roll with a rolling pin over the top, pressing down. You can also try crushing with the back of a heavy-based frying pan, (not to be hit hard from height!).

Manual Tools

If short of an electric grinder and a coffee grinder, herbs and spices can be crushed using a mortar and pestle.

Measuring

Always use clean, dry spoons for measuring so as not to contaminate or clog the contents.

Refrigeration
Curry powders, cayenne pepper and spice blends; such as chilli powder, paprika, red pepper will retain their flavour longer if kept refrigerated. Always refrigerate such spices in hot climates or in periods of hot weather.

Shelf-life
Check jars or bottles of crushed or ground herbs and spices, every 6-12 months. Although they don't 'go-off' in traditional terms, they will lose their aroma and flavour over time.

Spice Mixes
When making spice mixes, it's more economical not to make large amounts, due to its limited storage times. Opt instead to make smaller batches and use within 4-6 weeks for optimum taste, aroma and potency.

Storage Tips
Store herbs away from moisture and heat.

Store in a cool, dry place.
Spice racks and jars may look decorative on kitchen counters or walls, but for preservation of taste and aroma, they are much better stored in a cupboard, out of direct light and protected from kitchen heat and moisture.

Keep herbs and spices out of direct sunlight and away from cooking heat. Always screw the lid tightly on jars, or store fresh herbs and spices in an airtight container.

Mark bottles and jars with dates, so that you know when to check their freshness and replace them when necessary.

Where possible, store herbs and spices in glass bottles or jars. Plastic packaging is not completely airtight and the contents will lose their flavour very quickly in non-airtight conditions.

For optimum taste, replace dried whole herbs and spices annually and ground, crushed and powdered spices, every 6 months.

Tools & Cleaning Rituals

Keep your electric grinder pristine-clean; cleaning it thoroughly after each grinding session; and always cleaning it between grinding different herbs or spices. Extend the same treatment to your mortar and pestle too.

Whole Spices

Whole spices have a greater shelf-life than crushed, or ground forms. For longevity and taste, it is preferable to buy whole spices and crush, or grind them when required.

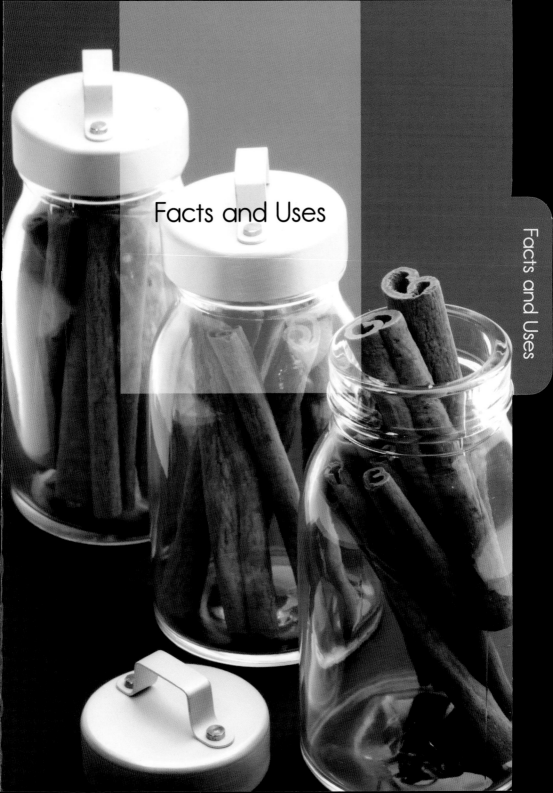

Facts and Uses

Allspice

Also known as pimento, Myrtle pepper, Jamaican pepper and newspice. The name 'allspice' suggests a combination of spices, but it is actually the dried fruit of the 'Pimento Dioica' plant, indigenous to the West Indies, Central America and Southern Mexico. Picked whilst unripe and dried in the sun, the fruits dry into dark, brown balls, similar to the size of peppercorns – they are then ground into powder for use. Its leaves can also be used for culinary purposes.

Culinary Uses

The distinctive aroma and taste of this spice is said to remind people of a blend of cinnamon, nutmeg and cloves; hence it's name, 'allspice'. It is popularly used in Caribbean and Middle Eastern cooking; as well as being an American and British culinary favourite.

A versatile and tasty spice, it can be used in a variety of foods and seasonings, such as; meats and fish, soups, stews and casseroles, marinades, chutneys, burgers, teas, barbeque and tomato based sauces, pies, cakes, biscuits and cookies.

Culinary Tip:
Allspice can be used as a substitute, (like for like), for cloves, nutmeg or cinnamon.

Medicinal Benefits
Allspice is believed to aid the body's digestive system and give relief to the symptoms of indigestion, trapped wind and flatulence.

Anise Seed

This flowering plant. (Pimpinella anisum), bears dry fruits, more commonly referred to as aniseed. This sweet, fragrant fruit produces a similar taste to liquorice and is used in a variety of both sweet and savoury dishes and beverages.

Culinary Uses
Savoury dishes include soups, stews and casseroles, curries, seasonings, sausages and sauces. Sweet dishes include biscuits, cakes, confectionary, (who didn't revel in sucking aniseed balls as a kid!), and pastries. It is also a well-known taste in a variety of international alcoholic drinks, such as Greek Ouzo, Turkish Raki, German Jagermeister, Italian Sambuca and a favourite of Parisian artists during the 19th Century, the 'Green Fairy' drink itself, Absinthe!

Culinary Tip:
Anise seeds will lose their distinctive flavour quite rapidly, so it's a good idea to buy the seeds whole and grind them when required. Always store in an airtight container, in a dry, dark place.

Medicinal Benefits
Available in seed and essential oil form, anise is reported to treat a number of health problems, such as; sore throats, colds and flu, toothache, menstrual pains, digestive discomfort, colic, hiccups, bad breath and containing anti-parasitic properties, it can also treat infestations of lice and scabies. In ancient times it was even used as an aphrodisiac!

Not to be used in pregnancy, unless used as food flavouring.

Arrowroot

Also known as the 'obedience plant', (Marantha arundinacea), this perennial herb originates in West India and is an edible starch.

Culinary Uses
Available in a similar-looking white powder as cornstarch, arrowroot can be used in puddings, jellies, ice cream, biscuits and cakes and is also a great thickener for sauces, fillings and puddings.

Culinary Tip:
Arrowroot will continue to thicken slightly, even when removed from the heat, so keep stirring the mixture for 1-2 minutes, just to remove the chance of lumps forming.

Medicinal Benefits
The absence of gluten in arrowroot flour makes it an excellent substitute in baking for those with an allergy or intolerance to gluten.

Basil (Sweet)

Amazingly, there are over 150 varieties of Basil! Sweet basil, (L.Ocimum Basilcum), comes from the mint family and is grown in warm, tropical climates - and as its name suggests, has a sweet, fragrant aroma.

The name 'basil' derives from the Greek word for 'king' – and is considered by some to be the 'king of herbs'.

Native to Africa, India and Asia, this spicy herb, with anise-like undertones and an aroma of cloves, has a long and controversial history.

Basil has literally been loved and hated in equal amounts all over the world! Considered as a sacred herb by the Hindus, considered in high esteem by the Indians and believed to be a symbol of love and fertility by the Romans; it was conversely loathed by the Greeks and in Europe during the Middle Ages, it was believed that scorpions bred under pots of growing basil – so just smelling a basil plant could result in the unsuspecting 'sniffer' forming a scorpion in the brain!

Culinary Uses

As probably the most commonly-known variety of basil, being traditionally associated with Italian cuisine, sweet basil is a culinary classic; used to flavour tomato-based soups and sauces, pasta and rice dishes, meats, vegetables, cheese dishes and green salads.

Culinary Tip:
When buying fresh basil, avoid buying basil that has black marks on or is wilting. For storage, freezing fresh basil and snipping off a few leaves when required is a good way to preserve freshness, whilst being economical at the same time.

Medicinal Benefits
Fresh basil contains folic acid and dried basil contains iron, calcium and potassium.

Its medicinal properties are said to aid digestion and assist in relieving digestive problems, such as; constipation, stomach cramps, nausea, motion sickness and vomiting.

Dried basil is also believed to be good for the respiratory system.

Bay Leaves

Also known as Bay Laurel, (Laurus nobolis), bay leaves come from the laurel tree, or sweet bay, and are predominantly grown in the Mediterranean. The leaves are green and glossy and they have a strong, sharp flavour.

In Ancient Greece and Rome, the branches were used in wreaths awarded to winners in sports and battles; and celebrated poets and artists. The Romans also believed that the tree protected them against plague and thunder.

Culinary Uses
Popularly used in Italian cuisine, the bay leaf's strong, astringent flavour makes it perfect for flavouring meats, sauces, soups, stews, poaching and braising liquids. They are also an important component in the French 'Bouquet Garni', a herb mixture commonly used in French cuisine.

Culinary Tip:
For best results, leaves should be slightly crushed before adding to cooking. The leaves are inedible and should always be removed before serving.

Medicinal Benefits
Bay leaves are thought to be good at soothing stomach complaints and also used as a remedy for rheumatism. Adding bay essential oil to a carrier oil is believed to soothe sore joints and muscles - or if you don't have the oil, add 2-3 bay leaves to a warm bath and soak as normal, this is said to soothe and calm the skin.

Referred to as the 'King of Spices', black pepper, 'Piper nigrum' is from the family 'Piperaceae'. The plant is cultivated for its fruit, (peppercorns), which are then dried and used as a spice, seasoning and condiment. Other fruits of 'Piper nigrum' produce white, pink, red and green peppercorns. Native to Southern India and used since prehistoric times, black pepper is one of the most common spices in European cuisine, often used as a condiment alongside table salt. Today it is primarily grown in India, Malaysia, Brazil and Indonesia. Historically, black pepper has been a much coveted spice, so much so that it was once a valuable trading good, used as a form of trading currency and nicknamed 'black gold'.

The demand for pepper even spurred on the Spanish explorations and spice trade in the 15th Century. In ancient Egypt, black peppercorns were used in the mummification of Ramesses II, suggesting it was a sacred spice.

Culinary Uses
This pungent and fiery spice is suitable for use with literally thousands of dishes! Complementing and seasoning; meats, marinades, chowders, soups, eggs, tomatoes, spice cakes, gingerbreads, sauces, pasta, cream cheeses, stews, casseroles, poultry… and much, much more.

Culinary Tip:
Black pepper is best purchased as whole peppercorns, as this offers a far more superior taste to ready-ground pepper. Whole peppercorns keep their flavour indefinitely. If stored correctly and are best ground directly onto food. Add towards the end of cooking for the best flavour.

Medicinal Uses
Black pepper has been utilised in a broad range of remedies in Indian medicine, such as; constipation, stomach problems, indigestion, insect bites, toothache and tooth decay, joint pain, liver and lung diseases, as well as heart disease. Today black pepper is recognised as a carminative, antibacterial, and stimulant. It is said to improve digestion, relieve stomach upsets, help reduce flatulence and calm the symptoms of nausea. Black pepper also works to raise body temperature, which is valuable for treating the chills.

Facts and Uses

Caraway Seeds

Caraway seeds are not actually seeds, but the fruit of the plant, 'Carum carv', a member of the parsley family. Originally native to Asia, Europe and parts of Africa, caraway seeds have been used as a spice as far back as the Middle Ages. Grown today in Holland, Germany, Russia, US, Canada and parts of Scandinavia, the seeds provide recipes with a strong, pungent aroma and a sweet but sharp taste, quite similar to anise.

Culinary Uses
Caraway seeds are popularly used as a spice for breads, particularly rye bread. They are also used in sauerkraut, sausages, pork dishes, casseroles, stews, soups, cheese dishes, potato salads, butters, liquors and liqueurs. Caraway seed also has a natural affinity with apples.

Culinary Tip:
Add in the last 15 minutes of cooking to optimise the taste, or even right at the end. Overcooking caraway seed can result in a bitter taste, not intended for the dish.

Medicinal Benefits
Caraway seeds are a natural carminative; a herbal remedy or preparation which prevents and helps to dispel gas from the gastrointestinal tract. Consequently, the seeds have been used in remedies for digestive and gastrointestinal disorders, such as colic, flatulence, appetite loss and irritable bowel syndrome.

Caraway seeds are also believed to have medicinal properties which will aid in treating the symptoms of respiratory illnesses such as; coughs, colds, sore throats and bronchitis.

Chewing caraway seeds is also said to dispel the smell of alcohol from the breath!

Cardamom

Native to India, Cardamom, (Elettaria cardamomum), is a derivative of the ginger family. Producing black and green varieties, the oval-shaped fruit pods are dried for use and are labeled as the 'Queen of spices'.

Ancient Egyptians used cardamom as a tooth cleaner, whilst the Romans and Greeks preferred it as a perfume. Cultivated today in countries, such as; Mexico, Thailand, Ceylon, Guatemala and Central America; this popular and expensive spice has an intense and highly aromatic, citrus-like flavour.

Culinary Uses
Traditionally used in Indian cuisine and an important ingredient in garam masala, Cardamom is also used in sweet dishes such as pastries, pies, yoghurts, creams and cakes. In Nordic countries cardamom is used in specialty breads and baking. In Arabic countries cardamom is familiarly used in coffee and tea, making a tasty, refreshing drink.

Culinary Tip:
When cooking the seeds, bruise them gently with the back of a knife before cooking; this will optimise the release of flavour.

Medicinal Benefits
Cardamom also has medicinal roots in herbal medicine; green cardamom can be used to treat throat infections, lung congestion, teeth and gum infections and also digestive ailments. Black cardamom is used in Chinese, Indian and Japanese medicine; often being used to treat digestive problems. It is also rumoured to be a powerful aphrodisiac.

Cardamom is often used as a mouth 'freshener' and its oils are also used in some perfumes.

Cayenne Pepper

Made from the dried pods of red-hot-chili-peppers, (from the Capsicum annum), Cayenne pepper is part of the nightshade family - and was historically misnamed as a 'pepper' instead of a spice, because of its pepper-like appearance. Named after the city of Cayenne in French Guiana, it is predominantly cultivated in the West Indies and Central and South America. The fruits are traditionally dried, ground and sifted into powdered form; Cayenne pepper.

Culinary Uses
This hot and pungent spice is popular in worldwide cuisines, including; Mexican, Italian, Middle Eastern, Asian and South American cooking. It can be used as both a spice and a condiment, complementing dishes such as; curries, seafood, soups, omelettes and soufflés, meats, chicken, stews, casseroles and sauces. It can also give a kick to pickles, chutneys and marinades.

Culinary Tip:
Cayenne pepper can easily overpower a dish when used as a condiment, so use sparingly.

Medicinal Benefits
Cayenne pepper has a number of medicinal properties; not least it's ability to quickly and effectively increase the body's circulation, which is good for warming the extremities and speeding up metabolism.

Cayenne is believed to be able to relieve pain and itching, as a gargling ingredient for sore throats and can be used for digestive ailments, such as stomach aches and cramps and trapped wind. Used topically, it is believed to relieve the symptoms of rheumatic and arthritic joint pains.

Chervil

From the plant 'Anthriscus cerefolium', chervil is a classic ingredient in the French herb blend 'Fines Herbes'. Originally native to southern Russia, this light green, fern-like-leaf herb was transported by the Romans to France, where it became, and remains, a staple herb in French cuisine. Chervil is familiar to Easter celebrations in parts of Europe, because its aroma is similar to that of myrrh and its spring-time growth is a symbol of renewal and regeneration.

Culinary Uses

Sometimes known as 'gourmet parsley', chervil is an aromatic and sweet herb, with a delicate hint of liquorice. Popular in French cuisine, chervil is used to flavour soups, stews, salads, omelettes, fish, poultry, creamy sauces, new potatoes, baby vegetables and cheeses. Chervil is the herb which gives Béarnaise sauce its distinctive taste.

Culinary Tip:
Add at the end of cooking or sprinkle on fresh chervil raw – overcooking will diminish the taste very quickly. Preserve in white wine vinegar to keep the flavour of fresh chervil.

Medicinal Benefits

As with many of the other herbs, chervil can be used to aid sluggish digestion and relieving stomach pains. It also has an impressive herbal remedy profile, being used for medicinal purposes, such as; improving circulation, relieving fluid retention, assists in clearing up eczema and acne, lowering blood pressure, helping bladder disorders and reducing varicose veins and cellulite.

Chives

Described as a 'herb spice', Chives, (Allium schoenoprasum), are members of the onion family and are predominantly grown in the Northern hemisphere. The bulbs produce bright green leaves, which shredded, are popularly used in cooking.

Chives grow together in 'clumps', (hence them being referred to them in the plural), and their flowers are a beautiful decorative addition to any garden. Chives have also been traditionally used in the garden for keeping away unwanted insects.

Culinary Uses
Grown for their leaves, rather than their bulbs, chives have a milder, more subtle flavour than onions and have a wide variety of culinary uses, such as in; soups, fish, pancakes, cheese dishes, sour cream sauces, eggs, butters and potato dishes.

In French cooking, chives are one of the 'Fines Herbes' a combination of chervil, tarragon, parsley and chives.

Culinary Tip:
Heat diminishes the flavour of chives, so care should be taken as to when they are added to a recipe.

Medicinal Benefits
Chives are rich with vitamins A and C and are known to lower blood pressure, which is beneficial to the body's circulatory system.

Cinnamon

Native to Sri Lanka, Cinnamon, (Cinnamomum verum), is an evergreen tree, of which the dried bark is used as a culinary spice. Popular even since ancient times, cinnamon was believed to be a sacred spice by the Romans and was often added to funeral pyres.

Cinnamon was once so sought after, that it was one of the predominant reasons for explorations during the 15th and 16th Centuries.

Cinnamon has a distinctive sweet, woody aroma, which can be purchased in ground, powdered form as well as cinnamon sticks, which are made from the bark of the tree by being rolled and pressed.

Culinary Uses

This warm spice is widely used in dessert dishes, baking and drinks, such as; chocolate, cookies, spiced fruits, pies, pastries, liqueurs, cocoa, teas, mulled wine, breads and sugars. It can also be used in savoury soups, stews and curry powders. In Middle Eastern and North African dishes, cinnamon is used to flavour lamb and stuffed aubergines.

Culinary Tip:
Be careful not to add cinnamon to boiling liquid, as this will impair the quality and taste.

Medicinal Benefits
Cinnamon has been traditionally used to treat health problems such as; colds, toothache, digestive ailments; such as flatulence, nausea and vomiting; and even bad breath.

It is high in antioxidants, which fight cell-damaging free radicals in the body.

Cloves

'Clove' is derived from the
Latin word for 'nail' – 'clavus'.
Documented as far back as 400BC,
cloves are a real Grandparent of the spices.
Native to Indonesia, cloves are the dried flower buds of the
aromatic, evergreen clove tree. The buds are small and reddish-brown in
colour and are picked whilst unopened and then dried. The trees also
grow in other tropical climates, including Jamaica, India, Brazil, Pakistan,
Sri Lanka and the West Indies.

Culinary Uses

Either ground or whole, this spice provides its dishes with a sharp and
piquant flavouring. Traditionally used in Indian cuisine, the strong, sweetly
pungent flavour is often combined with other spices in a plethora of Indian
dishes and drinks. Cloves are also commonly used in Mexican, North African
and Middle Eastern cuisine. Soups, stocks and stews will benefit from whole
cloves, (to be removed before serving), and to give sweeter dishes a deep,
spicy 'kick', cloves can be used, (sparingly), in cookies, cakes, muffins, syrups,
sweet sauces and gingerbread. Cloves are also used for mulling and
pickling spices.

Culinary Tip:

Cloves can easily overpower a dish, so always use sparingly, building up the
flavour gradually, if required. Grinding cloves manually is difficult, if not
almost impossible, (due to their hard exterior), so an electric spice grinder,
or coffee grinder is recommended.

Medicinal Benefits

Cloves are used in Chinese and Ayurvedic medicine, as well as Western
herbal traditions. The essential oil of cloves is used as a painkiller in dentistry
and can be used to treat health complaints such as indigestion, nausea,
vomiting, stomach aches and skin irritations. It's also believed that cloves
may reduce blood sugar levels. Cloves should be avoided by those
suffering with bowel disorders or gastric ulcers, as the strength of the spice
can irritate the mucosal layer of the gastrointestinal tract. Care should also
be taken in pregnancy.

Coriander (Cilantro)

Despite it's name in Greek, ('koris'), translating as 'bed bug'; coriander, the seed of the 'Coriandrum sativum'; is probably the one of the world's most widely used and popular herbs – and possibly the oldest, dating back to at least the second millennium BC. Traditionally used in Middle Eastern, Asian, Oriental and Latin American cuisine, this highly aromatic, annual herb belongs to the parsley family. Its recognition in European cuisine has increased over the last few decades and shows no decline.

Culinary Uses

The whole of the plant is edible, but the leaves and the dried seeds are most commonly used in cooking. The leaves, known as cilantro, are earthy and quite pungent, mostly used in savoury dishes, such as; soups, curries, stuffings, breads, chutneys, salads and as a popular garnish. The dried coriander seeds have a distinctly different citrus-like taste and can either be used whole or ground for culinary use. Coriander seeds are used in savoury dishes such as; meats, curries, seafood, sausages, chutneys, casseroles and soups – but they can also be used in sweet dishes, such as desserts, pies and pastries.

Culinary Tip:
Although coriander seeds and cilantro are from the same plant, their different tastes mean that they cannot be substituted for one another in recipes.

Medicinal Benefits
In Indian medicine coriander seeds are used as an ingredient in a diuretic remedy; and in holistic medicines, coriander is believed to promote the healthy functioning of the body's digestive system and can relieve an upset stomach or flatulence.

Coriander has also been used for the symptoms of anxiety.

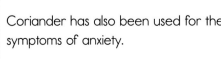

Cumin

Cumin is the dry seed of the herbaceous Cuminum cyminum plant, a member of the parsley family and native to the hot climates of the eastern Mediterranean and Egypt. Major suppliers of cumin include; India, Turkey, Iran and Pakistan. Historically, this ancient spice was a favourite flavouring in Roman cuisine; and during the Middle Ages, in Europe, it was believed that a marrying couple would have a happy life if they carried cumin during their wedding ceremony. It was also said to keep your lover from wandering! A very powerful spice indeed!

Culinary Uses

Cumin, 'Cuminum cyminum', has a strong, bitter flavouring and a warm and powerful aroma. The seeds are long and thin and come in three colours; white, black and amber. The black seeds have a distinctly different taste to the white and amber seeds, so are not interchangeable in recipes. Cumin can be used whole, for a more spicy-sweet flavouring, or ground, for a more bitter taste. Cumin is popular in a whole host of international cuisines, including; Mexican, Middle Eastern, Cuban, Asian, Turkish and Mediterranean cuisine. As a popular seasoning, cumin is the main ingredient in both curry powder and chilli powder; and can be used with spicy, savoury dishes, such as; meats, curries, chilli con carne, beans, enchiladas, tacos, chicken, fish, lentils and cheese dishes. Cumin is often combined with coriander and added to soups, stews, casseroles and rice dishes. Toasting the seeds will accentuate their flavour.

Culinary Tip:
To accentuate the cumin seed's earthy flavour and aroma, lightly dry-roast them before use.

Medicinal Benefits

Ancient medicine used cumin in the treatment of digestive problems, pain relief and tooth decay. In some herbal medicine remedies, cumin is believed to be effective in treating colds and respiratory problems and by making a tea from toasted cumin seeds and hot water, they are thought to soothe stomach aches, cramps and bloating. Cumin is also believed to be a stimulant, effective in the production of breast milk.

Facts and Uses

25

Dill (Seed & Weed)

Deriving from the perennial herb, 'Anethum graveolens', the seeds of the plant, known as dill seeds, are used as a spice; and the fresh leaves, known as dill weed, are used as a herb. Fresh green in colour and providing a refreshing and mild flavour, dill is an ancient herb, originating in Europe and Asia, (as far back as the Bible). Dill, which comes from the Norse word 'dilla', means to soothe, or lull. In ancient medicine it was used to soothe the stomach after meals, relieving bloating and gas – and for colic in babies. In ancient Greece it was considered a sign of wealth; and in Middle Age Europe, dill was believed to protect against the evils of witchcraft.

Culinary Uses

Dill is a popular addition to German, Scandinavian and Russian dishes, with the flavour of the leaves and seeds providing very different flavourings to recipes – for this reason they are not interchangeable with each other. The leaves (weed) are fragrant, with a clean, delicate and simple taste; good for flavouring foods such as; fish, shellfish, soups, cream sauces, mild cheeses, potato dishes, vegetables, (particularly cucumber), and dips. The seeds have a spicier, more potent flavour – similar to the caraway seed and anise and can be used whole or ground. Dill seeds are an excellent addition to food when sprinkled in or over casseroles, stews, soups, salads, rice dishes, root vegetables and salad dressings.

Culinary Tip:
Dill strengthens in taste during cooking, so use sparingly. Unlike some other herbs, dill will keep indefinitely if stored in a cool, dark place in an airtight container.

Medicinal Benefits
Still believed to have soothing and relaxing effects on the digestive system, herbal remedies using dill are used to relieve symptoms of gas, bloating, indigestion, nausea, colic and even hiccups! Dill is rich in vitamin C so aids in strengthening the immune system.

An ancient spice with supposed aphrodisiac powers, (it was certainly worth a mention in the Karma Sutra!); ginger is the underground stem of the ginger plant, 'Zingiber officinale'. With a long and colourful history, this sweet and pungent spice is a favourite of many international cuisines. In Medieval times it was used as a medicine against the plague and in the Philippines it is said to ward off evil spirits. Its origins are not certain, but the ginger plant is believed to be native to Asia.

Culinary Uses
Ginger is used in a variation of different forms:-

Ginger root, (fresh ginger): used as a potent spice in Indian, Chinese and Japanese cuisine, in dishes such as; curries, noodles, pickles, chutneys, pastes, seafood and spiced tea and coffee.

Dried ginger root (ground ginger / powder): used more traditionally as a spice for sweeter dishes, such as; gingerbread, cookies, candy, cake, ginger ale, ginger beer, ginger snaps, biscuits, jams and preserves.

Preserved or stem ginger, (fresh, young root): cooked in sugar syrup, then canned to make a hot and spicy confection, used in cakes, desserts and puddings.

Crystallised ginger: cooked in sugar syrup, air dried and rolled in sugar. Used in desserts, sweets, snacks and spiced teas.

Pickled ginger: traditionally used in Chinese and Japanese cuisine.

Culinary Tip:
Fresh ginger can be kept for several weeks, if correctly stored in the drawer of a refrigerator.

Ginger/continued

Medicinal Benefits

Used in Chinese medicine for centuries, ginger has an impressive portfolio of medicinal uses. Classified as a stimulant and carminative, ginger is known to improve circulation and digestion, settle the stomach, relieve the symptoms of colic, help indigestion and dyspepsia, nausea and stomach cramps. Ginger is believed to have anti-inflammatory properties, which can help with joint pain in arthritis. It also believed to cleanse the bowel and kidneys and remove toxins from the body. One of ginger's most popular uses is for the prevention of motion and morning sickness. Ginger helps to stimulate the production of saliva, making swallowing easier, which helps combat the unpleasant effects of nausea.

Marjoram

A herb which most either love or hate, Majorana hortensis or Origanum majorana, is also known as sweet marjoram. A derivative of the mint family and indigenous to the Mediterranean, this sweet and fragrant plant dates back to Greek and Roman times, who believed that it was a symbol of happiness. Belonging to the same family as oregano, marjoram has a delicate, mellow flavour with a hint of mint and citrus. Although delicate, it has a slight sharpness to it, so when used in cooking use sparingly.

Culinary Uses

Used largely in Italian and Mediterranean cuisine, marjoram is a great addition to soups, meats, poultry, stews, vegetables, eggs, cheeses, salad dressings, fruits, potatoes. It particularly complements red meat, such as lamb. Marjoram is also used in the herb blend, 'herbes de provence'.

Culinary Tip:
Best used fresh and at the end of the cooking process.

Medicinal Benefits

Marjoram has antifungal properties. Drinking marjoram tea is believed to relieve symptoms of ailments such as; stomach pain, coughs and colds, headache, indigestion, sinus congestion and hay fever. The leaves, if ground into a paste, are thought to relieve pain for sprains and rheumatism.

Mint

The mint plant, (Mentha) has literally hundreds of different varieties, the most significant of which being; peppermint (Mentha piperita L.) and spearmint (Mentha spicata). This fast-growing plant, native to Asia, is a popular culinary herb, with variable coloured leaves ranging from dark green to purple, to pale yellow. Used by the Romans to whiten teeth, it was also believed to symbolise hospitality.

Beneficial to gardens, the aromatic leaves repel unwanted insects and attract useful insects.

Culinary Uses

With a fresh, sweet flavour and a cool aftertaste, the leaves, (dried or fresh), are the culinary source of the plant.

Mint has a plethora of culinary uses including; teas, jellies, sauces, syrups, candy, ice cream, beverages, even alcohol - such as crème de menthe. Mint is a popular complement to lamb dishes in the UK.

Mint essential oil is also popularly used in breath fresheners, mouth washes, toothpaste, chewing gums, chocolate, cosmetics and perfumes.

Culinary Tip:
If you're a little overrun by your garden mint plant, use a little in table decorations – it looks attractive and is a great room freshener.

Medicinal Benefits
Mint is commonly used as a herbal remedy for stomach ache, to aid digestion, as a decongestant for colds, a refreshing pick-me-up and to relieve chest pains. It is a powerful diuretic and is effectively used to treat insect bites and stings. It is often used by the camping fraternity to repel mosquitoes and is also an eco-friendly insecticide.

Nutmeg

Despite the name, nutmeg is not a nut, but the egg-shaped seed of the tree, 'Myristica fragrans'. Cultivated in the West Indies, the tree is unusually also the source of another spice, mace. As a much sought after commodity, the procurement of nutmeg has been a cause of contention, smuggling and deception across the centuries. Believed to possess magical powers, such as attracting admirers and protecting wearers from evil, illness and bad luck – in addition to its culinary and medicinal properties - its reputation as a coveted spice is well documented. Nutmeg can be bought, whole, ground or in essential oil form. Its distinctive aroma and taste is described as sweet and nutty.

Culinary Uses

Particularly popular in the Netherlands and Italy, nutmeg can be used for a variety of savoury dishes, such as; curry powder, garam masala, soups, sausages, meats, potato dishes, cheese and cheese sauces and as a nutty-sweet addition to vegetables and lamb dishes. It is also a perfect baking, dessert and beverage spice for recipes including; fruit pies, puddings, desserts, custards, mulled wine and cider and alcoholic drinks. Nutmeg essential oil is commonly used in food flavouring for syrups, sweets, beverages and baking goods.

Culinary Tip:
The flavour of nutmeg diminishes quickly, consequently whole nutmegs, grated, are preferable to ground nutmeg.

Medicinal Benefits

Nutmegs are poisonous, so should be used in moderation. In small doses, nutmeg aids digestion, treats vomiting and nausea, relieves flatulence and can improve appetite. Indian herbal medicine used nutmeg in remedies to treat headaches, fever and bad breath. Nutmeg essential oil is often in used in the pharmaceutical industry, for products such as cough mixture, ointments and toothpaste. It is also used in the cosmetic industry.

Oregano

Mediterranean Oregano, (Origanum vulgare L.), translated into Greek means 'Joy of the mountains'. Used prolifically in Greece, Italy and in Italian-American cuisine, this pungent herb produces a number of varieties, specific to where the plant is cultivated. Oregano is a relation of marjoram and produces a warm, slightly bitter taste. It is a classic ingredient in the herb blend, 'Bouquet Garni'. The leaves are used as a culinary ingredient and surprisingly, the dried herb is more flavourful than the fresh herb itself.

Culinary Uses
Oregano is popularly used in Italian cuisine to add flavour to tomato sauces, pizzas, salad dressings and vegetables. It is also a staple in Greek cuisine, traditionally cooked with lamb and Greek salad. Oregano complements dishes with lemon and garlic and is a flavour-rich addition to red meats, fish, pork, chicken, Moussaka and hot, spicy dishes.

Culinary Tip:
Oregano has a strong taste, so should be used sparingly in order to avoid overpowering the dish.

Medicinal Benefits
Oregano leaves are high in antioxidants and work as a powerful antiseptic, carminative and antispasmodic. In herbal remedies they are used to treat colds, flu, fevers, stomach upsets, indigestion and menstrual pain.

Paprika

Paprika is a spice produced by grinding the pods from dried green and red peppers, from the family, Capsicum anuum. Paprika comes in different varieties, depending on the type of peppers used; ranging from sweet bell peppers to spicier chilli peppers. Believed to be native to South America and introduced to Spain by Christopher Columbus, this lively spice is popular in Mediterranean, South American and eastern European cuisine. Traditionally associated with Hungarian cuisine, such as Hungarian goulash and chicken paprikash; paprika is also used in a broad variety of dishes, worldwide. Paprika is currently predominantly cultivated in South America, Spain, Hungary and California.

Culinary Uses

Ranging from a deep red colour to brown, the peppers used vary in taste and heat depending on the variety and area of cultivation; from sweet, mild and slightly smoky, to full bodied and piquant. Paprika can be used to flavour and colour rice, stews, tomato sauces, casseroles, marinades, fish, soups, sausages, (such as chorizo), meats, potato salads, egg and cheese dishes. It can be smoked to provide a deeper flavour and mixed with breadcrumbs to sprinkle over vegetables or casseroles. Fresh paprika deteriorates quickly, so is best purchased in small quantities and kept it in a cool, dry place in an airtight container. Ground paprika is available from most supermarkets and convenience stores.

Culinary Tip:
Take care when heating paprika, as it burns easily, which makes the spice taste bitter. Add only with liquid ingredients and do not heat over a high heat for too long

Medicinal Uses

Paprika is rich in vitamin C, providing seven times more vitamin C than oranges – although the cooking process will diminish the quality of vitamins. A good source of beta-carotene, (which converts to vitamin A), paprika also has antibacterial properties and acts as a stimulant, making it beneficial for the body's circulation, digestion and blood pressure.

Parsley

Parsley, (Petroselinum crispum) is one of the more well-known and popular herbs. It has a number of varieties, the most common being the flat leafed Italian parsley and curly parsley. The two have distinctly different tastes, so are attributed in different ways for culinary use, e.g. curly parsley is commonly used as a garnish, whereas flat leaf parsley has a stronger, more pungent flavour. As an ancient herb, parsley has an eventful history; the Greeks used parsley to crown their 'victors' at their games events and the Romans believed that wearing a wreath made of parsley would prevent inebriation, by absorbing the alcoholic fumes. Parsley also has historical links to the occult.

Culinary Uses
Parsley is a versatile herb, with a mild, fresh aroma and a slightly peppery, but not overpowering, taste. Popular in Central and Eastern Europe and West Asia, fresh, chopped parsley is often sprinkled over dishes for extra taste. Parsley is a congenial flavouring for a broad range of dishes, such as; potato dishes, vegetables, rice, fish, soups, chicken, lamb, steaks, stews, green salads, dips, sauces, stocks, omelettes and butters; it is also part of the French herb blends 'fines herbes' and 'Bouquet Garni'.

Culinary Tip:
Dried parsley is best bought in smaller amounts, as its flavour and colour diminish quite rapidly. When picking dried parley, search out deep-green 'flakes', with no yellow leaves and unwanted stalks.

Medicinal Uses
Parsley is a nutritious herb, high in vitamins C and A, also containing amounts of copper, iron and iodine. Herbal remedies are used to balance blood pressure and can be used as an effective diuretic.

Rubbed onto the skin, parsley is believed to reduce the itching of mosquito bites. Parsley, chewed raw, is an excellent breath freshener and is supposed to negate the pungent smell of garlic on the breath

Parsley should not be used as a herbal remedy or supplement by pregnant women, due to possible stimulant effects.

Native to the Mediterranean and a member of the mint family, rosemary, from the Latin 'Rosmarinus' , translates into English as 'Dew of the Sea' – due to the complementary conditions for its growth by the coast. The herb comes from the small evergreen shrub, Rosmarinus officinalis. Legend has it that the Virgin Mary, fleeing from Herod, draped her blue cloak on a rosemary bush, laying a white flower on top. In the morning the flower had turned blue, as a consequence the bush was then dubbed the 'Rose of Mary'. In ancient Greece it was believed that rosemary strengthened the function of the brain and revitalised the memory, so much so that students wore springs of rosemary in their hair during examinations. Rosemary was also associated with remembrance, due to its enhancement of the memory and was often worn and/or burned at funerals and weddings.

Culinary Uses
Rosemary has a slightly astringent, pine-like taste with an aromatic fragrance. The flavour is best retained as whole 'needles', but it can also be bought dried and chopped for ease of chewing. Used predominantly in Mediterranean cuisine, rosemary complements dishes such as; roasted meats, (traditionally used with lamb), poultry, stews, tomato sauces, marinades, roasted vegetables and potatoes, soups and fish.

Culinary Tip:
Rosemary can range from mild to fairly pungent in taste, so when cooking it's best to use it sparingly and build up to the desired flavour, so as not to overwhelm the dish.

Medicinal Benefits
Rosemary is a carminative and effective stimulant, used in herbal remedies for ailments such as indigestion, flatulence, dyspepsia, stomach upsets, nervous problems, headaches and colds. It also has anti-inflammatory and antiseptic properties and is used as a gargling remedy to heal mouth ulcers and cankers – as well as a breath freshener. Rosemary oil is said to relieve muscular and arthritic pain and its stimulant properties improve circulation. Fresh rosemary, crushed and added to bath water is thought to soothe aching muscles. Medical research has shown a decrease in breast tumours, (in laboratory experiments), in relation to the consumption of rosemary.

Facts and Uses

Saffron, derived from the dried stigmas of the saffron crocus flower, 'Crocus sativus', is notoriously the world's most expensive spice, with over 22,000 stigmas needed to produce just one pound of this precious commodity. Native to the Mediterranean and Western Asia, it is aptly nicknamed, 'The Golden Spice', and has been coveted for thousands of years; with documented use stretching back over 4,000 years. The name, saffron, originates from the Latin word 'Safranum' meaning, 'yellow'. In its freshly picked form, the stigmas are threadlike orange strands, with a strong, hay-like fragrance. In addition to being used as a flavouring and colouring for food, saffron was largely used for its medicinal properties, treating a whole range of gastrointestinal illnesses, wounds and even parasite infestations. Greek courtesans used saffron in their ointments, perfumes and potpourris; and both the Romans and Greeks liberally scattered saffron to perfume public baths. In India saffron was used to mark members of wealthy castes, to show their superiority.

Culinary Uses
Good quality saffron is deep red in colour and emits a rich, heady aroma. The taste is warm and delicate, but slightly bitter and spicy. Its addition to food provides an attractive golden-yellow colouring. Just a pinch will give the desired colour, which is fortuitous given its expense! Saffron is often used for its colouring properties in Indian dishes and desserts. It is also used in Spanish paella, Italian risottos, Middle Eastern dishes, French bouillabaisse, Scandinavian sweetbreads, confectionaries and alcoholic drinks.

Culinary Tip:
To achieve an even distribution and to avoid overwhelming the dish, steep a pinch of freshly crushed saffron in hot water before adding to the cooking.

Medicinal Benefits
Known to have anti-carcinogenic, antioxidant and anti-inflammatory properties, saffron is said to treat a variety of ailments including; indigestion, dyspepsia, flatulence, arthritic pain, menstrual pain, kidney and bladder disorders and poor circulation. It is also believed to be increase serotonin levels in the brain, assisting in combating the symptoms of depression. Large quantities of saffron are known to be fatal.

Facts and Uses

Sage

Sage, the Latin 'salveo' meaning 'to save' is a well-known herb from the evergreen shrub, 'Salvia officinalis'. An established member of the mint family, there are a few hundred different types of sage. The most commonly used variety being silvery-grey in colour and sporting a strong, slightly musky aroma and a pine-like, woody flavour. Dating back as far as ancient Rome, the Romans heralded sage as a sacred herb, which was used during planting and harvesting ceremonies for prosperity and good luck. In folklore, sage was a symbol of wisdom, enhanced memory, longevity and virtue – hence the term 'an old sage', meaning an old, wise person.

Culinary Uses

Sage is famous for its culinary contribution to sage and onion stuffing, used for poultry dishes, but it is also a savoury complement to pork, veal, sausages, potatoes, seafood, soups, stews, savoury scones and muffins and even speciality cheeses and teas. The chopped leaves are an excellent addition to salads, chutneys and pickles; and work as an attractive garnish for soups and stews.

Culinary Tip:
Sage is a potent herb, which could easily overpower a recipe if not appropriately used. When adding to any recipe, use sparingly and increase the quantity, little by little, if required.

Medicinal Benefits

Traditionally believed to have powerful healing and medicinal properties, with antiseptic and antibacterial properties, sage has a strong history of medicinal application. Its consumption was said to purify the blood and rubbed directly onto the teeth and mouth, it was used to clean and freshen the breath. It was also used as a gargle for sore throats, mouth ulcers and sore gums and in baths, soothed aching limbs and rheumatic pain.

Tarragon

Known also as the 'dragon herb', from the small shrub, 'Artemisia dracunculus L.', tarragon is part of the sunflower family. The origin of the name, tarragon, is somewhat ambiguous, but is possibly a play on the

French word 'estragon', which means 'little dragon'; believed to be named so due to the plant's roots curling, like a dragon's tail. There are two varieties of tarragon cultivated, French and Russian, however the most commercially used tarragon comes from the dried leaves of the French tarragon plant. Native to Russia and Western Asia, tarragon was used in the Middle Ages to treat dog bites and as an antidote for poisonous snake bites.

Culinary Uses

Tarragon is a healthy green colour, with a bittersweet, peppery flavour and a slight aroma and taste of anise. It is traditionally associated with vinegar and fish dishes. Popular in French cuisine, tarragon is one of the traditional ingredients in the French herb blend 'Fines Herbes' – and a main ingredient in Béarnaise sauce. It is also a complementary flavouring when used in vinegars, dressings, pickles, relishes, mustards, cream sauces, sour cream, yoghurt and butters; as well as an accompaniment for dishes such as; fish, meat, seafood, chicken, soups and stews, vegetables, tomato, cheese and egg dishes. In parts of Eastern Europe, tarragon is added to carbonated soft drinks as a refreshing beverage.

Culinary Tip:
Tarragon that has been stored in vinegar is far more flavourful than dried tarragon.

Medicinal Benefits

Although not popularly used in modern herbal medicine, tarragon has historically been used as a digestive aid, for relieving stomach cramps, flatulence and as an appetite stimulant. Chewing tarragon causes numbness in the mouth, due to it having slight anaesthetic properties, (eugenol), – thus, the ancient Greeks used tarragon as a temporary remedy for toothache. Tarragon is believed to speed up the body's natural elimination process, getting rid of toxins from the body and is a mild diuretic.

Thyme, 'Thymus vulgaris' was a symbol of courage in ancient Greece and Roman soldiers bathed in an infusion containing thyme, to bring courage, invigoration and strength. Indigenous to the Mediterranean, this tiny-leafed herb with grey-green leaves; is a member of the mint family and is cultivated in several different varieties. Regular thyme is most popularly marketed and sold, but for a different taste try using lemon thyme for a zesty kick.

Culinary Uses
The leaves are dried, then chopped or ground for culinary use, providing a subtle and fresh aroma, with a slight hint of mint to its taste. A versatile and much-used herb, thyme is an essential ingredient in the French herb blend, 'Bouquet Garni'.

Thyme's taste complements most meats, soups, sauces, vegetables, stews, pasta sauces, poultry, seafood, chowders, eggs and tomato-based dishes.

Culinary Tip:
Good quality thyme will contain very little twig or stalk. When adding a whole sprig, make sure that it's not too 'woody' as this will take on a bitter taste, which will be detrimental to the dish.

Medicinal Benefits
Thyme has an impressive portfolio of medicinal uses under its belt, having been utilised as a battlefield antiseptic and painkiller during World War I. Thyme is believed to improve digestion, by assisting the digestion of fats and it's also believed to stimulate the lungs, encouraging the expulsion of mucous and relieving unpleasant congestion.

Its antiseptic qualities are said to fight off bacterial and viral infections and used as a gargle remedy, thyme is thought to combat dental decay, bad breath, oral thrush and mouth ulcers. Thyme has even been used as part of a hangover remedy!

Turmeric derives from the root of the 'Curcuma longa', which is part of the ginger family. Native to Southeast Asia, turmeric has long been used as a condiment and dye; dating back more than 4,000 years. Today, India is the main producer of turmeric, with other cultivations being grown in countries such as; China, Peru, Sri Lanka, Jamaica and Indonesia. As well as its culinary uses, turmeric is also used to dye clothing in India. And if you're wanting to rid yourself of ants in your garden or house, just lay down some turmeric, for some unknown reason they can't stand the stuff!

Culinary Uses

Ground into a bright orangey-yellow coloured powder, turmeric is often known as the poor man's saffron; as it is a less expensive way of obtaining a similar, yellow food colouring. With an earthy, warm and vaguely mustardy aroma, turmeric provides a peppery, slightly musky taste and is probably best known for being the classic spice ingredient in curry powder and its extensive use in Indian cuisine. Popular in Middle Eastern and Southeast Asian cooking, turmeric is used as both a flavouring and colouring for a foods, such as; pickles, relishes, mustards, lentils, rice and meat dishes, soups, salad dressings, desserts, cakes, jellies, juices, sauces, dry mixes and fish.

Culinary Tip:
Turmeric is a pungent spice, which gets stronger during cooking, so use sparingly and adjust accordingly. As a powerful yellow dye, take care not to touch your clothing whilst cooking – it can be difficult to remove completely once stained.

Medicinal Benefits
Turmeric has long been known as having valuable medicinal properties and past and present, has been accredited with having high anti-inflammatory properties, as well as containing antiseptic and antibacterial agents. It is also considered to be a stimulant, digestive aid, a carminative and antispasmodic. Turmeric has been used in herbal and other holistic and alternative medicines to treat ailments such as; cuts and burns, digestive complaints, stomach cramps, staphylococcal infections, toothache, menstrual pain, colic and chest pains. It has also been linked with the possible prevention of certain cancers, liver disorders and neurodegenerative diseases.

Facts and Uses

Vanilla

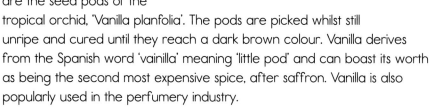

Originating in Mexico and discovered by the Aztecs, who used it as a flavouring in a cocoa drink, vanilla was eventually transported to Europe during the 16th Century. Today it is grown in Mexico, Tahiti, Madagascar and Indonesia. Vanilla beans are the seed pods of the tropical orchid, 'Vanilla planfolia'. The pods are picked whilst still unripe and cured until they reach a dark brown colour. Vanilla derives from the Spanish word 'vainilla' meaning 'little pod' and can boast its worth as being the second most expensive spice, after saffron. Vanilla is also popularly used in the perfumery industry.

Culinary Uses

Good quality vanilla should have a strong, aromatic flavour with a delicate smoky and sweet taste. There are three preparations readily available when purchasing vanilla; whole pod, ground powder or extract, (soaked in alcoholic solution). Vanilla is a widely used and popular flavouring, predominantly in deserts and other sweet dishes and beverages, such as; ice-cream, custards, cake, candy, puddings, sauces, yoghurts and in liqueurs such as, Galliano and Crème de Cacao.

Culinary Tip:
When purchasing vanilla beans, look for oily flexible pods for good quality. Vanilla extract is very strong, so a few drops in the required dish or beverage should be more than enough.

Medicinal Benefits

Unfortunately, vanilla does not have any proven medicinal benefits and is not used as such. Although, it was once believed to be an aphrodisiac and a cure for impotence. It was also once used to reduce a fever, but this use has long since been rendered unbeneficial.

Starters and
Snacks

Aubergine Fritters (Serves 8)

2 tsps garam masala
6 aubergines (sliced)
250g/2 1/4 cups of plain flour
2 eggs
300ml/1 1/3 cups of milk
2 tbsps salt
Oil (for deep frying)

1. Sprinkle the sliced aubergines with salt and leave to drain for 30-35 minutes. Place the eggs, milk, flour and garam masala in a bowl and beat together until a smooth batter, (or place in a food processor and blend for 30 seconds).

2. Rinse the aubergine slices in cold water and pat dry with kitchen paper. Dip each slice in the batter and deep fry in the oil for 8-10 minutes. Remove from the oil and drain on paper kitchen towel. Serve immediately.

Carrot & Coriander Soup (Serves 4)

2 tsps ground coriander
1-2 tbsps coriander leaves (chopped)
50g butter
4-6 tbsps single cream
2 small onions (sliced)
450g carrots (diced)
300ml/1 1/3 cups of orange juice
900ml/4 cups of chicken stock
Salt and black pepper (to season)

1. Heat the butter in a large saucepan and add the onions. Cook the onions for 3-4 minutes, until tender. Add the carrots and cook for a further 2-3 minutes. Add the chicken stock, ground coriander and orange juice and bring just to the boil. Reduce the heat, cover and simmer for 45-50 minutes.

2. Transfer the soup, (in batches), to a food processor and return to the saucepan. Re-heat and ladle into serving bowls. Garnish each bowl with a swirl of cream and sprinkle over a little coriander.

Cheese & Herb Bread Italian-Style

1/2 tbsp dried basil
1/2 tbsp dried oregano
1/2 tbsp salt
1 clove of garlic (crushed)
400g/3 1/2 cups of white bread flour
35g/1/3 cup of Romano cheese (grated)
1 tbsp caster sugar
225ml/1 cup of warm water
2 tbsps olive oil
8g baking yeast

1. Place the sugar, yeast and warm water in a large bowl and mix together. Leave to one side for 5-7 minutes, until the mixture froths. Add the basil, oregano, grated cheese, garlic, oil, salt and half of the flour and mix together well. Once combined, add the remaining flour, little by little, and mix together to make a stiff dough.

2. Remove the dough from the bowl and knead for 6-8 minutes. Grease the inside of a bowl with oil and place the dough inside, turning it so that the whole outside of the dough is oiled.

3. Cover the bowl with a clean, damp cloth and leave from 1 hour. Grease a baking tray in preparation.

4. Once the dough has risen, press the dough down to release any air. Shape the dough into a loaf and place on the baking tray. Leave for 30 minutes, to allow the loaf to double in size.

5. Preheat the oven to 180C/350F/Gas mark 4. Place the loaf in the oven and bake for 30-35 minutes, until risen and golden.

Cheese & Parsley Stuffed Mushrooms (Serves 4)

2 tsps parsley flat leaf
1/4 tsp garlic salt
4 large flat mushrooms
1 tbsp olive oil
75g/3/4cup of Cheddar cheese (grated)
2-3 spring onions (chopped)
Salt and black pepper (to season)

1. Preheat the grill to a medium setting. Brush the mushrooms with the olive oil and season with salt and black pepper, according to taste. Place under the grill, (gill side down), and cook for 4-5 minutes.

2. Place the grated cheese, garlic, parsley and spring onions in a bowl and mix together well. Remove the mushrooms from under the grill and turn them over. Fill the insides with the cheese, parsley and onion mixture and return to the grill.

3. Cook for a further 5 minutes and then serve immediately. Serve with a rocket and tomato salad.

Cinnamon-Spiced Fruit Couscous (Serves 8)

2 tsps cinnamon
2 cups of instant couscous
75g/1/2 cup of raisins, or sultanas
1/2 cup of almonds (slivered)
45g/1/4 cup of pitted dates (finely chopped)
450ml/2 cups of smooth orange juice
335ml/1 1/2 cups of water

1. Place the orange juice and 1 cup of water in a saucepan and bring to the boil. Remove from the heat. Add the couscous to the saucepan and cover with the lid. Leave for 5 minutes, (or as per packet instructions).

2. Place the raisins, dates, cinnamon, almonds and 1/2 a cup of water in a saucepan and heat for 2-3 minutes. Add the couscous and mix together well. Serve immediately.

French Toast with Herbs (Serves 2-4)

3/4 tbsp parsley (finely chopped)
1 tbsp chives (finely chopped)
1/2 tbsp thyme (chopped)
1/8 tsp paprika
4 eggs
4 tbsps milk
1 tbsp sunflower oil
4 slices thick, white bread (cut into triangles)
Salt and black pepper (to season)

1. Place the herbs, eggs, milk and paprika in a bowl and mix together well. Season with salt and black pepper, according to taste. Place to one side.

2. Heat the oil in a frying pan and dip 3/4 of each of the triangles in the herbed batter (covering both sides). Carefully drop into the frying pan and cook for 1-2 minutes on both sides, until golden brown.

3. Serve immediately with your bacon, mushrooms and eggs. Sprinkle over with a little chopped parsley, if desired.

Greek Salad (Serves 2)

1/2 tsp oregano
1/2 tbsp fresh mint (chopped)
125g/1 cup of feta cheese (roughly chopped)
1/2 Cos lettuce (shredded)
1/2 cucumber (deseeded & chopped)
4 tomatoes (deseeded & chopped)
1/2 red onion (finely sliced)
100g/1 cup of black olives (pitted)
1 tbsp capers (finely chopped)
1 tbsp red wine vinegar
55ml/1/4 cup of virgin olive oil
Black pepper (to season)

1. Place the capers, olive oil, red wine vinegar and oregano in a bowl and mix together well. Place the chopped onion, cucumber and tomatoes in a bowl and combine well.

2. Add half of the caper dressing and toss well, coating all the ingredients. Cover and refrigerate for 20 minutes.

3. Remove from the refrigerator and add the shredded lettuce and olives. Toss the salad gently before transferring to a serving dish. Place the feta cheese in the bowl with the remaining dressing and gently toss. Sprinkle the feta over the salad and season with ground black pepper. Top with chopped mint to serve.

Lentil and Onion Soup (Serves 4-6)
1 tsp cumin seeds
12g/1/4 cup of coriander leaves (chopped)
1/2 tsp ground turmeric
1 inch fresh ginger (peeled & finely chopped)
1 yellow onion (finely chopped)
900ml/4 cups of chicken stock
2 tomatoes (chopped)
225ml/1 cup of milk
55g/1/4 cup of unsalted butter
250g/1 1/4 cups of dried red lentils (picked through & rinsed)
Salt and freshly ground black pepper (to season)

1. Place the lentils in a large saucepan, followed by the chicken stock, chopped tomatoes, ginger and turmeric. Bring to the boil, reduce the heat and simmer for 20-25 minutes, until the lentils are tender.

2. Remove from the heat and transfer the soup, (in batches), into a food processor. Blend until smooth and return to the saucepan. Stir in a little salt and milk and re-heat. Simmer gently over a low heat.

3. Melt the butter in a frying pan and add the onion; cook for 1 minute and then add the cumin. Cook for
4-5 minutes, stirring frequently.
Add the onion/cumin mixture
to the soup. Season with
black pepper and sprinkle
over chopped coriander.

Mackerel Pate with Dill (Serves 8-10)
2 tbsps dried dill
1/2 tsp ground white pepper
1/2 tsp garlic salt
450g smoked mackerel (skin & bones removed)
2 egg whites (stiffly beaten)
2 tsps lemon juice
300ml/1 1/3 cup of double cream (lightly whipped)
1/2 - 1 cucumber (sliced – to garnish)

1. Place the mackerel in a bowl and add the lemon juice, dill, garlic salt and pepper. Mash the ingredients together well with a fork. Stir in the cream and mix well, followed by the egg white. Ensure that all the ingredients are combined together well and mashed.

2. Spoon the mixture into a large serving dish and place in the refrigerator overnight. When ready to serve, remove from the fridge and garnish with slices of cucumber.

Nectarine and Basil Bagels (Serves 4)
Approximately 20 basil leaves
4 bagels
4 thinly sliced nectarines
8 tbsps low-fat cream cheese
1/2 tbsp cracked black pepper

1. Split and toast the bagels, spreading them with cream cheese. Top each bagel with the nectarine slices and basil leaves. Sprinkle lightly with black pepper and serve.

Savoury Herb Scones (Serves 16)

2 tbsps sage
1 large egg (beaten)
300ml/1 1/3 cup of milk
460g/4 cups of self raising flour
3/4 tsp salt
65g butter (softened)
2 tsps baking powder
Pinch of black pepper

1. Preheat the oven to 230C/450F/Gas mark 8. Place the sage and milk in a bowl and mix together. Leave to stand for 6-8 minutes. Place the required number of baking trays in the oven and heat through.

2. Sift the baking powder, flour, salt and black pepper into a bowl and rub in the butter, until the mixture becomes like fine breadcrumbs. Gradually add the milk/sage mixture, stirring continuously.

3. Flour a clean work surface and turn out the dough from the bowl. Knead the dough gently and then roll it out to 2cm thick. Using a shaped cutter, cut out the required number of scones and brush over the top with the beaten egg. Place the scones on the heated baking trays and place in the oven for 10-12 minutes, until risen and lightly browned.

Serve warm with preferred cheeses, pickles or chutneys.

Spiced Fried Cauliflower (Serves 6)

1 tsp chilli powder

1 tsp cumin

1 tsp coriander

1 tsp turmeric

1 tbsp fresh coriander (chopped)

18 cauliflower florets and stalks (cooked)

150g/1 1/3 cups of plain flour

1/8 tsp salt

1/2 lime

Vegetable oil (to fry)

Sparkling mineral water (to mix)

1. Sift the flour and spices into a bowl and mix together. Make a well in the middle of the mixture and add a little of the sparkling water.

2. Mix in well and continue to add until the mixture is like a thick paste. Set aside for 40 minutes. Add the stalks to the batter, mixing and coating them well.

3. Heat about 4cm of vegetable oil in a pan and add the cauliflower stalks. Fry for 3-4 minutes until the stalks are nice and crispy. Transfer onto a serving dish and sprinkle over with the chopped coriander and a squeeze of lime juice. Serve immediately as a snack, or accompaniment.

Main Meals

Beef in a Warm Bean Salad (Serves 3-4)

1/2 tsp dried chilli flakes
1/2 tsp dried oregano
300g/2 cups of cooked beef
370g/6 cups of canned cannellini beans
1 red onion (chopped)
1 clove of garlic (crushed)
Olive oil (to serve)
1 tbsp balsamic vinegar (to serve)
Salt and black pepper (to season)

1. Preheat the oven to 200C/400F/Gas mark 6. Place the beans, chopped onion, garlic, chilli flakes and oregano in a baking dish and combine well.

2. Cover with foil and place in the oven for 25-30 minutes, until the beans are tender. Remove from the oven and leave to cool a little for 2-3 minutes.

3. Drizzle over some olive oil and sprinkle the balsamic vinegar; mix into the beans gently. Lay the sliced beef over the beans and serve with warm crusty bread.

Chicken Biryiani (Serves 4)

5 whole cloves
2 cinnamon sticks (crushed)
18 green cardamom pods
1 tsp cumin seeds (crushed)
1 tsp coriander seeds (crushed)
Handful coriander leaves (chopped)
1 tsp saffron powder
1/2 tsp rock salt
3 cloves of garlic (finely chopped)
2 inches fresh ginger (peeled & sliced)
5 tbsps ghee
2 onions (sliced)
1 green Serrano chilli (seeded & finely chopped)
50g cup of dried mango pieces
40g/1/4 cup of sultanas

Chicken Biryiani/cont.

75g/1/2 cup of pistachio nuts (blanched & skinned)
2 1/2 lbs chicken (cubed into 4 equal pieces)
560ml/2 1/2 cups of chicken stock
335g/1 1/2 cups of basmati rice

1. Place the chicken stock, chilli pepper, salt, cinnamon, ginger and chicken pieces in a large, heavy saucepan. Bring to the boil. Reduce the heat, cover and simmer for 30 minutes. Remove the chicken and place to one side. Pour the cooked liquid into a large measuring jug and measure 2 1/2 cups; add water if required.

2. Heat the ghee to the saucepan and add the onion. Fry for 3-4 minutes, until golden brown. Remove the onion with a slotted spoon and keep to one side. Add the cloves, cardamom pods and basmati rice to the saucepan and stir-fry for 2-3 minutes. Add the chicken pieces, followed by the mango, raisins, garlic, pistachios, cumin, saffron and crushed coriander seeds. Cook the mixture for 2-3 minutes, stirring continuously.

3. Pour the stock back into the saucepan and bring to the boil. Reduce the heat, cover and simmer for 13-15 minutes, until the rice is tender and the liquid has been absorbed. Sprinkle the chopped coriander leaves over the top and serve immediately.

Cinnamon & Ginger Chicken with Cranberries (Serves 8)

1/2 tsp ground ginger
1/2 tsp ground cinnamon
8-10 chicken breasts (skinless)
200g/2 cups of fresh cranberries
2 onions (chopped)
450ml/2 cups of orange juice
6 tbsps honey
1 tsp salt
3 tbsps flour (mixed with 2 tbsp cold water)

1. This recipe is to be cooked in a slow cooker. Cook at a low temperature. Place all of the ingredients, (except the flour mixture), in the slow cooker and gently mix.

2. Cover and cook for 7 hours, until the chicken is cooked through. Stir in the flour mixture and cook for a further 20 minutes, or until the mixture has thickened. Serve with a choice of vegetables.

Chicken & Herbs in Cider (Serves 6)
2 bay leaves
2 tbsps fresh tarragon (chopped)
1 tbsp fresh parsley (chopped)
6 chicken breasts (skinless)
450g shallots (whole)
4 cloves of garlic (peeled, but not sliced or crushed)
500ml/2 1/4 cups of dry cider
335g/1 1/2 cups of crème fraiche
2 tbsps vegetable oil
Salt and black pepper (to season)

1. This is another recipe to be cooked in a slow cooker. Place the shallots in a large bowl and pour over with boiling water, enough to cover them. Leave to stand for 15 minutes. Drain and peel off the skins. Heat the vegetable oil in the frying pan and add the shallots (whole). Fry gently for 8-10 minutes until lightly browned. Cook at a low temperature.

2. Add the garlic and fry for a further 3 minutes. Remove from the heat and transfer the garlic and shallots to the slow cooker (do not pour in the oil.) Place the frying pan and oil back over the heat and add the chicken. Cook for 3-4 minutes until lightly browned on both sides. Place the chicken over the shallots and garlic in the slow cooker.

3. Add the cider and bay leaves to the frying pan and bring to the boil. Season with salt and black pepper, according to taste. Pour the cider into the slow cooker. Cover and cook for about 5 hours until the chicken and shallots are cooked.

Chicken & Herbs in Cider/continued

4. Remove the chicken breasts from the slow cooker and keep warm. Stir the herbs and crème fraiche into the cider mixture in the slow cooker and mix well.

5. Return the chicken breasts to the slow cooker and cook on a high temperature for a further 30 minutes. Remove the bay leaves and garlic cloves before serving.

Cream & Herb Fettuccini with Salmon (Serves 4)
1/4 tsp oregano
1/4 tsp basil
1/4 tbsp fresh parsley (chopped)
335g/1 1/2 cups of cooked salmon (skinned & boneless)
225ml/1 cup of single cream
75g/1 cup of mushrooms (sliced)
250g/2 1/2 cups of fettuccine pasta
150g/3/4 cup of tomatoes (chopped)
2 tbsps chopped onions
1 tbsp flour
2 tbsps butter
75g/1/2 cup of frozen peas (thawed)
Salt and black pepper (to season)

1. Cook the pasta, as per the packet instructions. Heat the butter in a large frying pan and add the onions and mushrooms. Cook for 4-5 minutes, stirring frequently. Stir in the flour until well mixed, followed by the cream. Bring to the boil; reduce the heat and simmer, stirring continuously, for 1-2 minutes.

2. Add the peas, salmon, parsley and tomato and season with salt and black pepper. Cook for 3-4 minutes, stirring occasionally. Drain the cooked fettuccine and return to the pan. Pour in the salmon mixture and gently combine. Serve immediately.

Fish Curry (Serves 2)

1/2 tsp ground cumin
1/2 tsp chilli powder
1/2 tsp ground coriander
1/2 tsp ground turmeric
1/2 tsp ginger paste
1 bay leaf
250g/1 1/4 cup of cooked cod fillets (cut into chunks)
1/2 onion (chopped)
1 fresh green chilli (chopped)
1 clove of garlic (crushed)
65ml/1/4 cup of natural yoghurt
75ml/1/3 cup of water
2 tbsps vegetable oil
Salt (to season)

1. Heat the oil in a large frying pan and add the onion. Cook for 3-4 minutes, until tender. Add the garlic, bay leaf and ginger and cook for 1 minute.

2. Stir in the spices and continue to cook for another minute. Pour in the yoghurt, followed by the chilli and water. Bring to the boil, reduce the heat and simmer for 3 minutes.

3. Add the cod pieces and season with salt. Cover the pan and simmer for 15 minutes. Remove the bay leaf before serving. Serve with hot, cooked rice.

Hot Beef & Potato Supper (Serves 2)

2 tsps paprika
1 tbsp fresh chives (chopped)
225g/1 1/2 cups of rump or sirloin steak (cut into 1 inch long strips)
170g/3/4 cup of cooked new potatoes (halved)
1 red onion (sliced)
300ml/1 1/3 beef stock (hot)
70g/1/3 cup of cherry tomatoes (halved)
1 clove of garlic (crushed)
30g/1/4 cup of plain flour
1 tbsp vegetable oil
Splash of Worcestershire sauce
Salt and black pepper (to season)

1. Place the flour in a bowl and add the paprika, mix together well. Toss the strips of beef in the mixture, coating them well and place to one side. Heat the vegetable oil in a large frying pan and add the coated beef strips. Cook for 3-4 minutes, stirring occasionally to brown all sides of the meat.

2. Add the garlic, potatoes and onion and continue to cook for 3 minutes. Add the beef stock, cherry tomatoes and Worcestershire sauce and season with salt and black pepper, according to taste. Cook for a further 2-3 minutes.

3. Adjust seasoning, if required and sprinkle over with chopped chives. Serve hot with warm, crusty bread and a choice of vegetables.

Lamb Curry (Serves 3-4)

1 bay leaf
2 cardamom pods
1/2 tsp turmeric
1/2 tsp chilli powder
1/2 inch ginger (grated)
350g/3 1/3 cups of cooked lamb (cubed)
2-3 potatoes (peeled & quartered)
450ml/2 cups of water
1 onion (sliced)
2 cloves of garlic (crushed)

3 tbsps vegetable oil
1/2 tbsp vinegar
1/2 tsp salt

1. Heat the oil in a large pan and add the potatoes. Cook for 4-5 minutes, until browned. Remove with a slotted spoon and leave to one side. Place the cardamom pods and bay leaf in the pan and cook for 10 seconds. Add the garlic, ginger and onions and cook for 3-4 minutes, until browned.

2. Add the turmeric, salt, vinegar and chilli and cook for a further 1-2 minutes. Stir in the lamb, coating the cubes well with all the spices. Cook for 4-5 minutes.

3. Pour in the water and bring to the boil. Reduce the heat, cover and simmer for 35-40 minutes, stirring occasionally. Add the potatoes, re-cover and cook for a further 15-20 minutes, until tender.

Lamb Kofta (Serves 2-3)
2 tbsps fresh mint
2 tbsps fresh coriander
1/2 tsp cumin
265g/1 3/4 cups of cooked lamb (roughly chopped)
1 egg
2-3 tbsps vegetable oil
Salt and black pepper (to season)
Tzatziki (to serve)
Pitta breads (to serve)

1. Place the lamb in a food processor and blend until finely chopped. Add the coriander, mint, cumin and egg. Season with salt and black pepper, according to taste. Blend again until the ingredients are finely chopped and well mixed. Wet both hands and divide the mixture into equally sized balls, (approx. 8-10).

2. Heat the vegetable oil in a non-stick frying pan and add the lamb kofta balls. Cook over a medium heat for 3-4 minutes, each side. Remove from the pan with a slotted spoon. Place on paper kitchen towel to drain off any excess fat. Serve with Tzatziki, warmed pitta breads and side salad.

Lemon & Herb Pork Chops (Serves 4)

1 tsp oregano
1 tsp thyme
4 pork chops (trimmed of fat)
3 tbsps lemon juice
Black pepper (to season)
1 tbsp olive oil

1. Place the chops in a glass baking dish and add the lemon juice, oregano, thyme and a sprinkle of black pepper. Make sure that the chops are all covered with the mixture and leave to marinate for 20 minutes.

2. Place the olive oil in a frying pan and heat over a medium heat. Add the chops and cook for approx. 10 minutes, turning once. Cooking times may vary, depending on the thickness of the chops. Serve with choice of vegetables.

Mixed Roast Vegetables with Herbs

3 sprigs of fresh thyme
3 sprigs of fresh rosemary
900g/2 lb mixed root vegetables, such as; sweet potatoes, carrots, swede, parsnips, potatoes (peeled & cut into large chunks)
200g/7 oz whole shallots (peeled)
2 tbsps olive oil
1 tsp rock salt
1 tsp fresh black peppercorns

1. Preheat the oven to 220C/425F/Gas mark 7. Place all the vegetables in a saucepan and cover with boiling water. Bring to the boil, reduce the heat and simmer for 6-7 minutes.

2. Drain the vegetables and place in an appropriately sized roasting tin. Brush the vegetables with the oil and sprinkle over with salt and black peppercorns.

3. Evenly place the herb sprigs in the roasting tin and place in the centre of the oven. Roast for 35-40 minutes, turning halfway through cooking. Remove from the oven when golden brown and crisp. Serve immediately.

Nice 'n' Spicy Chicken Burgers (Serves 2)

1 tbsp fresh coriander (chopped)
1/2 tsp fresh ginger (crushed)
1 chilli (deseeded & finely chopped)
250g/2 cups of cooked chicken
125g/2 1/2 cups of breadcrumbs
1 egg
1 tbsp vegetable oil
Salt and black pepper (to season)

1. Place the chicken in a food processor and blend until finely chopped. Add the ginger, chilli, egg, coriander and breadcrumbs and blend until the mixture is smooth. Season with salt and black pepper, according to taste. Lightly sprinkle flour over a clean work surface.

Nice 'n' Spicy Chicken Burgers/continued

2. Transfer the contents of the processor to a bowl and using wet hands, divide the mixture into balls. Lightly flatten the balls into a burger-shape.

3. Heat the vegetable oil in a frying pan and add the chicken burgers. Cook for 8-10 minutes, until golden brown on both sides, ensuring that the burgers are heated through thoroughly.

Serve immediately with a side salad and potato wedges.

Red Lentil Curry (Serves 2-3)
1 tsp curry powder
1/2 tsp chili powder
1 tsp turmeric
150g/2 cups of canned red lentils (drained & rinsed)
1 onion (chopped)
1 clove of garlic (crushed)
1 1/4 pint of vegetable stock
1-2 tbsps olive oil

1. Heat the oil in a saucepan and add the onions. Cook for 4-5 minutes, until tender. Add the spices and garlic and stir well. Add the red lentils and 3/4 of the vegetable stock. Bring to the boil.

2. Reduce the heat and simmer for 25-30 minutes, until the lentils are cooked. Add more stock throughout, if needed. Serve with hot cooked rice and/or Naan breads.

Roasted Spiced Salmon (Serves 2)
1 tsp chili powder
1/4 tsp paprika
1/2 tsp cumin
Ground black pepper
2 salmon fillets (uncooked)
Juice of 1/2 lemon

1. Preheat the oven to 220C/425F/Gas mark 7. Line a baking tray with baking paper and spray with low-fat cooking spray. Place the spices in a small bowl and mix together well.

2. Place the salmon fillet, (skin side down), on the baking tray. Sprinkle over the spices and then rub them gently. Squeeze the lemon juice over the fillet and sprinkle lightly with ground black pepper.

3. Place in the oven for 10-12 minutes, (per inch of fillet thickness). Remove from the oven when the fish flakes easily with a fork.

Salmon & Tarragon Risotto (Serves 8)
3 tbsps fresh tarragon (chopped)
900g salmon fillets (skinned & diced)
Bunch of spring onions (finely sliced)
450g/2 cups of easy-cook Arborio rice
280ml/1 1/4c ups of white wine
3 litres/6 1/2 cups of vegetable stock
1 small cucumber (peeled & chopped)
3 tbsps butter (melted)
Salt and black pepper (to season)

1. To be cooked in a slow cooker. Cook at a high temperature. Add the melted butter to the slow cooker, followed by the chopped spring onions and cucumber. Cover and cook for 25-35 minutes.

2. Stir in the rice, followed by the white wine and vegetable stock. Re-cover and cook for 45 minutes, stirring halfway through cooking. Stir in the salmon and season well with salt and black pepper.

3. Re-cover and cook for a further 15 minutes, until the rice and salmon are cooked. Stand for 5-10 minutes, open and gently stir in the tarragon. Serve immediately.

Sausage & Vegetables in Spicy Rice (Serves 4)

1/2 tsp cayenne pepper
1/2 tsp dried thyme
1 tbsp fresh coriander (chopped)
250g cooked sausages (chopped into small pieces)
110g/1/2 cup of streaky bacon (chopped)
150g/1 cup cooked vegetables, such as; broccoli, peas, peppers, courgettes, green beans, etc (chopped)
300g/1 1/3 cups of long grain rice
1 onion (finely chopped)
280g/4 1/2 cups of canned kidney beans (drained & rinsed)
2 cloves of garlic (crushed)
375ml/1 can of coconut milk
1/2 tsp Encona hot sauce or Tabasco sauce (according to taste)
450ml/2 cups of boiled water
Salt and black pepper (to season)

1. Heat a large non-stick frying pan and add the bacon. Cook for 2 minutes, then add the garlic and onion. Cook for a further 2-3 minutes.

2. Add the chopped sausage, kidney beans, coconut milk, herbs, hot sauce and cayenne pepper. Bring to the boil and cook for 1-2 minutes, stirring continuously.

3. Add the rice and boiling water. Reduce the heat, cover and simmer for 25 minutes, until cooked. Stir in the leftover chopped vegetables and season with salt and black pepper, according to taste. Serve in individual serving bowls, with a sprinkling of coriander.

Seafood Jambalaya (Serves 4)

1 tsp dried thyme
1 tsp dried oregano
2 bay leaves
1 tsp cayenne pepper
225g/8 oz haddock (boned, skinned & cubed)
115g/4 oz cooked prawns
110g cooked chicken (diced)
6 rashers of streaky bacon (chopped)
750ml/3 1/3 cups of hot vegetable stock
1 onion (chopped)
2 cloves of garlic (crushed)
4 tomatoes (skinned & chopped)
2 celery sticks (chopped)
1 green pepper (deseeded & chopped)
300g/ 1 1/3 cups easy-cook rice
1 tbsp tomato puree
2 tbsps vegetable oil

1. To be cooked in a slow cooker. Heat the oil in a frying pan and add the bacon. Cook for 2-3 minutes. Add the onion, pepper and celery and cook for a further 6-8 minutes, until softened. Pour into the slow cooker.

2. Add the tomato puree, hot vegetable stock, thyme, oregano, garlic, cayenne pepper and bay leaves to the slow cooker and stir together well. Cover and cook on a high heat for 1 hour.

3. Add the rice to the slow cooker, followed by the haddock pieces. Season well with salt and black pepper and re-cover; continue to cook for 40-45 minutes.

4. Stir in the prawns and cook for a further 15 to 20 minutes, until the fish and rice are tender, (do not overcook the rice).

Spicy Turkey Meatballs (Makes 14)

1 tsp ground cumin
1 tsp chili powder
50g/2 cups of fresh coriander (finely chopped)
220g/1 3/4 cups of turkey mince
1 onion (finely chopped)
1 jalapeno pepper (finely chopped)
1 egg white
45g/1/3 cup of dry breadcrumbs
4 tbsps milk

1. Preheat the oven the 200C/400F/Gas mark 6. Spray a baking tray with low-fat cooking spray. Place all the ingredients in a large bowl and mix together well with a fork. Once mixed, make approximately 1½ inch meatballs and place them on the baking tray.

2. Place in the oven and bake for 20 minutes, turning them over once half-way through cooking. Remove from the oven and transfer to a frying pan, with approximately 2-3 cups of marinara sauce (see below).

Marinara Sauce

1 tbsp dried oregano
1/2 tbsp dried basil
900g/4 cups of canned chopped tomatoes
900g/4 cups of sieved tomatoes (such as passata)
110g/1/2 cup of tomato puree
225ml/1 cup of dry red wine
3 cloves of garlic (crushed)
2 tbsps olive oil
1 green pepper (finely chopped)
Salt & black pepper (to season)

1. Heat 2 tablespoons of olive oil in a frying pan and add the garlic and chopped green pepper. Cook for 2-3 minutes, until slightly browned. Transfer to a large saucepan or casserole dish. Add the chopped and sieved tomatoes, tomato puree, herbs, red wine and season with salt and black pepper and cook on a very low heat either on the hob (saucepan) or in the oven for 1-1 1/2 hours.

Sauces, Dips & Dressings

Basil & Spring Onion Mayonnaise

75g fresh basil (chopped)
1 tsp black pepper
1 large egg
1 tsp lemon juice
2 tbsps spring onions (chopped)
1 tsp salt
225ml/1 cup of olive oil

1. Combine the egg, lemon juice, basil, spring onions, salt and pepper in a food processor and blend until pureed. Gradually add a little of the olive oil and blend each time.

2. Scrape the sides of the processor and blend again, ensuring that all the ingredients have been successfully pureed.

3. Transfer the mayonnaise into an airtight container and refrigerate for at least 1 hour before serving. Use within 24 hours.

BBQ Seasoning

50g/1/2 cup of sweet paprika
110g/1/2 cup of dark brown sugar
110g/1/2 cup of sea salt
4 tbsps ground black pepper

1. Place all of the ingredients in a bowl and whisk together, until well combined.

2. Store in an airtight glass jar and store in a cool, dry and dark place. Use within 6 months.

Bouquet Garni

4 tbsps dried thyme
4 tbsps dried bay leaf
45g/1/2 cup of dried parsley
4 tbsps dried rosemary (optional)

1. Place the thyme, parsley, bay leaf and rosemary in a bowl and combine together. Place in an airtight container and store in a cool, dry place. Use within 6 months of making.

When added to a recipe for flavouring, tie the combined herbs inside cheesecloth; this will make the bundle easier to remove before serving.

Cajun Seasoning

1/8 cup of salt
1/8 cup of chilli powder
1/8 tsp white pepper
1/8 tsp cumin
1/8 cup of paprika
1 tsp dried thyme
1/4 tsp cayenne pepper
1/4 tbsp ground coriander
1/4 tbsp dried oregano
1/4 tbsp basil
1/4 tbsp black pepper
1/4 tbsp onion powder

1. Place all of the ingredients in a bowl and combine together well. Place the mixture in a glass, airtight container and store in a cool, dry place. Use within 3-4 months of making.

Use to spice up dishes, such as; chicken, BBQ ribs, pastas, fish, sauces and soups.

Chervil Pesto
70g/1 cup of fresh chervil
1 clove of garlic (crushed)
25g/1/4 cup of pine nuts (toasted)
25g/1/4 cup of Romano cheese
3 tbsps olive oil

1. Place all of the ingredients in a food processor and blend until chopped and blended.

Preferably use the pesto immediately, or store in an airtight container and refrigerate. Use with 3 days.

Cold Curry Sauce
1 tsp turmeric
1/2 tsp ground cumin
1/2 tsp ground coriander
2 egg yolks
300ml/1 1/3 cups of light olive oil (or sunflower oil)
2 tbsps lemon juice
300ml/1 1/3 cup of natural yoghurt
Salt and black pepper (to season)

1. Place the egg yolk, turmeric, cumin and coriander in a food processor and blend for 5 seconds.

2. Whilst the processor is running on a low speed, drizzle in the olive oil slowly. Once mixed, turn the processor off.

3. Add the yoghurt and lemon juice and blend for 8 seconds. Season with salt and black pepper, (according to taste). Transfer into a pouring jug and serve with cold chicken or fish.

Cream Cheese & Caraway Seed Spread

1 1/2 tsps caraway seed
75g/1/3 cup of cream cheese
35g/1/3 cup of blue cheese (crumbled)
75ml/1/3 cup of mayonnaise
Pinch of white pepper

1. Blend all of the ingredients together and transfer into an airtight container. Place in the refrigerator and use within 3 days.

Creole Spice

30g/1/3 cup of dried thyme
35g/1/3 cup of sweet paprika
30g/1/3 cup of dried basil
2 1/2 tbsps cayenne pepper
2 tbsps chilli powder
2 tbsps gumbo file powder

1. Place all of the ingredients in a bowl and whisk together, until well combined. Store in an airtight glass jar and store in a cool, dry and dark place. Use within 6 months.

Five-Spice Seasoning

6 whole cloves
2 cinnamon sticks (broken into small pieces)
2 tsps fennel seeds
2 tbsps black peppercorns
3 star anise

1. Dry-toast the peppercorns in a frying pan, over a medium heat, for 1-2 minutes. Move the pan continuously, to prevent the peppercorns from burning. Remove from the heat and transfer to a bowl. Repeat the process for the remaining spices. Leave to cool completely.

2. Transfer all of the toasted spices into a spice grinder and grind into a fine powder. Leave for 2 minutes. Transfer the spice mix to a glass, airtight container and store in a cool, dry place. Use within 4-6 weeks.

French 'Fines Herbes'

1 tbsp dried parsley
1 tbsp dried chervil
1 tbsp dried tarragon
1 tbsp dried chives

1. Place all of the ingredients in a bowl and whisk together, until well combined.

2. Store in an airtight glass jar and store in a cool, dry and dark place. Use within 4 months. If using fresh herbs, chop and combine together well. Add to recipes at the end of the cooking process.

Fresh Basil Dressing

1 handful of fresh basil leaves (chopped)
Juice of 1 lemon
395ml/1 3/4 cups of olive oil
Salt and black pepper (to season)

1. Blend all of the ingredients in a blender, until smooth. Transfer to a bottle and cover. Refrigerate and used when required.

Garam Masala

1 whole nutmeg (grated)
1 tsp whole cloves
1/4 cup of coriander seeds
2 tsps cardamom pods
2 tbsps cumin seeds
2 cinnamon sticks (broken into pieces)
1 tbsp black peppercorns

1. Heat a frying pan and dry-toast the coriander seeds for 2 minutes, continually moving them around the pan, ensuring that they don't burn. Remove from the pan and place in a bowl.

2. Repeat this process with the peppercorns, cardamom, cinnamon, cloves and cumin seeds. Allow all of the spices to cool completely.

Garam Masala/continued

3. Place all of the roasted ingredients into a spice grinder and grind into a fine powder. Pour out into a bowl and sprinkle the grated nutmeg over the top. Stir in well. Transfer the finished spice-mixture to a glass, airtight container. Store in a cool, dry place and use within 4-6 weeks.

Herbs de Provence
1 tsp dried basil
1 tsp rosemary
1/2 tsp dried sage
1/2 tsp fennel seeds
3 tbsps dried marjoram
3 tbsps dried rosemary
2 tbsps dried savory

1. Place all of the ingredients in a bowl and whisk together, until well combined. Store in an airtight glass jar and store in a cool, dry and dark place. Use within 4 months.

Hot & Sour Fish Chilli Sauce
1 tbsp coriander root (chopped)
2 tbsps fresh coriander leaves (chopped)
85g/1/3 cup fresh red chillies (stalks removed)
85g/1/3 cup fresh fresh green chillies (stalks removed)
1 tbsp fish sauce
1 tbsp lemon juice
2-3 cloves of garlic
1 tbsp vegetable oil
1 onion (chopped)
2 tbsps shallots (finely chopped)

1. Heat the oil in a frying pan and add the chillies, sauté for 1 minute and then remove with a slotted spoon. Place to one side. Add the onion, coriander root and garlic and cook for 3-4 minutes. Remove from the heat.

2. Transfer the onion mixture and chillies to a food processor and blend for 5-8 seconds - do not puree. Transfer to a bowl and stir in the fish sauce

and lemon juice. Add a little hot water if the sauce is too thick. Stir in the chopped shallots and coriander leaves and serve immediately.

Hot & Spicy French Dressing
1/4 tsp ground cayenne pepper
1 tsp paprika
1 tsp dry mustard
75ml/1/3 cup of chilli sauce
1 tsp salt
1/2 tsp black pepper
2 tsps horseradish (optional)
115ml/1/2 cup of fresh lemon juice
340ml/1 1/2 cups of olive oil
3 cloves of garlic (crushed)

1. Place all of the ingredients in a large jar, screw on the lid and shake well. Refrigerate and used when required.

Humus (Serves 4-6)
2 cloves of garlic (crushed)
8 tbsps water
3 tbsps lemon juice
2 tsps ground cumin
1 tbsp extra virgin olive oil
400g can of chickpeas (drained & rinsed)
200g/7 oz tahini
1 1/2 tsp paprika
1/2 tsp salt

1. Place the chickpeas, garlic, cumin, lemon juice, tahini, salt and water in a food processor and blend until creamy.

2. Spoon out into a serving bowl and smooth over with the back of a spoon. Drizzle with olive oil and sprinkle over paprika. Serve with pitta bread and olives

Italian Herb Dressing
6 fresh basil leaves
2 sprigs of fresh thyme
2 sprigs of fresh rosemary
2 sprigs of fresh oregano
340ml/1 1/2 cups of extra virgin olive oil

1. Place all of the herbs in a 350ml bottle and using a funnel, pour in the olive oil. Cover tightly and refrigerate. Use within 3-4 days.

Jerk Seasoning
1 tsp ground allspice
2 tsps dried thyme
2-3 tsps Encona hot pepper sauce or Tabasco
2 tbsps soy sauce
3 cloves of garlic (crushed)
6 spring onions
55ml/1/4 cup of fresh lime juice
55ml/1/4 cup of olive oil

1. Place all of the ingredients in a food processor and blend until the mixture becomes a paste. Transfer into a dish and rub over your choice of meat, chicken or fish before cooking.

Lamb & Pork Marinade
1 handful of crushed thyme
2 tbsps smoked paprika
4 cloves of garlic
8 tbsps olive oil
2 tbsps sherry vinegar
Salt and black pepper (to season)

1. Combine all of the ingredients in a bowl with a pestle and mortar, until smooth.

Lemon Dill Vinaigrette
1/2 cup of chopped fresh dill
110ml/1/2 cup of lemon juice
2 tbsps Dijon mustard
400ml/1 3/4 cups of olive oil
Salt and black pepper (to season)

1. Whisk the lemon juice and mustard together in a bowl. Gradually whisk in the oil, followed by the dill.

2. Season with salt and black pepper and leave to stand at room temperature for several hours, to allow the flavours to infuse.

Lemon & Herb Butter
1 tsp oregano (chopped)
1 tsp basil (chopped)
1 tsp parsley (chopped)
1 tbsp lemon zest (finely grated)
110g/1/2 cup of butter

1. Place all of the ingredients in a bowl and mix together.

2. Once the ingredients are well combined, pack into blocks and refrigerate for at least 1 hour before use.

Mexican Spice
1 tbsp ground cumin
2 tsps dried oregano leaves
50g/1/2 cup of chilli powder
1 tsp garlic powder
1 tsp ground dried chilli pepper
25g/1/4 cup of paprika
1 tsp onion powder
1/2 tsp salt

1. Place all of the ingredients in a bowl and whisk together, until well combined. Store in an airtight glass jar and store in a cool, dry and dark place. Use within 3 months.

Mint & Yoghurt Dip
1 tbsp dried mint
2 tbsps olive oil
310g/1 1/4 cup of strained yoghurt
Juice of 1 lemon
Salt and black pepper (to season)

1. Place the yoghurt, mint, salt and black pepper in a bowl and mix together. Add the olive oil and lemon juice, whilst stirring continuously. Combine well. Transfer to a serving dish, cover and refrigerate for 1-2 hours before serving.

Parsley Dip
1 large bunch of parsley leaves
1 clove of garlic
1 slice of bread
1 onion (sliced)
2 tbsps olive oil
310g/1 1/4 cup of strained yoghurt
Juice of 1 lemon
Salt & black pepper (to season)

1. Soak the bread in water, strain and place in a food processor. Add in the parsley, onion, garlic, salt and pepper and blend together.

2. Transfer to a bowl and stir in the olive oil, yoghurt and lemon juice; combine well. Spoon into a serving dish and cover.

Refrigerate for 1-2 hours before serving.

Red Pepper & Herb Dressing
2 tbsps fresh mint (chopped)
3 tbsps fresh oregano (chopped)
3/4 tsp ground black pepper
1 clove of garlic (crushed)
55ml/1/2 cup of extra virgin olive oil
115g/3/4 cup of red onion (finely chopped)
115g/2/3 cup of red pepper (finely chopped)

55ml/1/4 cup of fresh lemon juice
2 tsps salt

1. Place all of the ingredients in a large jar, screw on the lid and shake well. Refrigerate and used when required.

Satay Sauce
1 tbsp lemon grass (chopped)
1/2 tsp ground cumin
1/2 tsp ground coriander
1 tsp chilli powder
2 tsps tamarind juice
2 cloves of garlic
1 onion (finely chopped)
1/2 tsp shrimp paste
125g/1/2 cup of crunchy peanut butter
250ml/1 1/8 cup of coconut milk
1 tsp vegetable oil
2 tbsps sugar
Salt (to season)

1. Place the onion, lemon grass, shrimp paste, chilli powder, garlic, cumin and coriander in a food processor and add some of the coconut milk, just enough to wet the ingredients.

2. Gently heat the oil in a saucepan and add the mixture to the pan. Stir fry the mixture, until a pale pink-brown colour. Pour in the remaining coconut milk, stirring continuously and cook over a low heat.

3. Add the peanut butter, stirring briskly. Once the peanut butter is mixed in, add the tamarind juice, sugar and a pinch of salt. Take care not to burn the sauce.

4. If too thick, add a little more coconut milk – or if too thin, simmer gently until sufficiently reduced.

Tarragon Dressing
1/2 tsp fresh tarragon (finely chopped)
2 cloves of garlic (crushed)
170ml/3/4 cup of olive oil
1 tbsp red wine vinegar
1 tbsp mustard
Juice of 1 lemon

1. Blend all of the ingredients in a blender, until smooth. Transfer to a bottle and cover. Refrigerate and used when required.

Tarragon, Lemon & Leek Vinaigrette
3 tbsps dried tarragon
110ml/1/2 cup of lemon juice
1 egg yolk
2 tbsps Dijon mustard
3 tbsps tarragon vinegar
1 leek (finely minced)
340ml/1 1/2 cups of vegetable oil
225ml/1 cup of extra virgin olive oil
Salt and black pepper (to season)

1. Whisk the egg yolk and mustard together in a bowl. Whisk in the lemon juice and vinegar.

2. Place the tarragon and leek in a bowl and mix together until well combined. Stir into the lemon juice/vinegar mixture.

3. Gradually pour the oils into the mixture, whisking continuously, until mixed in. Season with salt and black pepper.

Tarragon Vinegar
Sprigs of fresh tarragon
225ml/1 cup of white wine vinegar
1 tsp salt
1/2 tsp sugar
Handful of dry-roasted peppercorns

1. Mix the vinegar, salt, sugar and peppercorns together and add the tarragon. Store in an airtight bottle and steep the tarragon for at least 1 month before use.

Tzatsiki
2 cloves garlic, finely minced
1 tbsp chopped fresh dill
1/4 olive oil
2 tbsps vinegar
500g/3 cups plain yogurt
1/2 cucumber peeled, seeded, diced cucumber
Salt and black pepper to taste

1. Blend all the ingredients together well then chill. Serve as a dip with sliced pitta bread.

Walnut & Basil Pesto
1 handful of fresh basil
1 handful of fresh flat-leaf parsley
200g/2 cups of toasted walnuts
1/4 tsp dried chilli flakes
2 cloves of garlic
75ml/1/3 cup of extra virgin olive oil
Juice of 1 lemon
Salt and black pepper (to season)

1. Place all of the ingredients, except for the oil and lemon, in a food processor. Pulse the food several times until the ingredients are 'crumbly'.

2. Transfer the ingredients into a bowl and drizzle the olive oil in, in one continuous stream, stirring throughout. Stir in the lemon juice and adjust seasoning, if desired.

Butter Bean & Herb Dip (Serves 2)

1 tsp fresh coriander (finely chopped)
1 tsp fresh parsley (finely chopped)
1 clove of garlic (crushed)
2 tbsps olive oil
150g/2 cups of canned butter beans (drained & rinsed)
Juice of 1 1/2 lemons
Salt and black pepper (to season)
4 slices of bread (crusts removed)

1. Preheat the oven to 150C/300F/Gas mark 2. Place the lemon juice, garlic, herbs and butter beans in a food processor and season with salt and black pepper. Add 1 tablespoon of olive oil and blend the mixture.

2. To create a thick and creamy dip, add a little more olive oil, if needed. Transfer into a serving bowl.

3. Grill the bread under a medium grill for 2-3 minutes, turning halfway through. Lay the slices of bread on a baking tray and place in the oven until the bread dries out and is crunchy – do not burn.

Serve the dip with the warm toast.

Something sweet!

Something sweet!

Allspice & Chocolate Slices (Serves 10-12)

2 tsps ground allspice
16 digestive biscuits (crushed)
55g/1/4 cup of glace cherries (chopped)
50g/2/3 cup of slivered flaked almonds
100g/3/4 cup of dark chocolate (melted)
55g/1/4 cup of butter (melted)
1 tbsp orange juice

1. Place the biscuits, almonds, allspice and cherries in a bowl and mix together well. Add the orange juice, melted butter and chocolate.

2. Transfer the mixture to shallow cake tin and spread evenly, smoothing the surface with the back of a spoon.

3. Refrigerate for 2-3 hours, (or longer if preferred), until set. Cut into slices and serve.

Anise Star Cookies (Makes 24)

1/4 tbsp star anise
140g/1 1/4 cups of plain flour
150g/2/3 cup of caster sugar
2 egg whites
Pinch of bicarbonate of soda

1. Grease 2 baking trays with butter. Sift the flour into a bowl and place to one side.

2. Place the egg whites in a bowl and whisk, until thick and fluffy. Carefully fold in the caster sugar.

3. Add the anise and bicarbonate of soda to the flour and combine well. Fold carefully into the egg/sugar mixture.

4. Fill a nylon icing bag with the mixture, fitted with a star shaped nozzle and pipe onto the baking trays. Leave the cookies to dry for at least 8 hours, (or overnight), and then bake at 150C/300F/Gas mark 2 for 15-20 minutes, until golden.

Baked Cinnamon Apples & Raisins (Serves 6-8)

2-3 tsps cinnamon
6-8 medium to large apples (cored)
3 clementine oranges (peeled, sectioned & chopped)
75g/1/2 cup of golden raisins
1/4 cup of cold water

1. This recipe should be cooked in a slow cooker, but if you do not have one, cook in a conventional oven on the lowest heat possible. Place the chopped orange sections, raisins and cinnamon in a bowl and mix together.

2. Stuff the cored apples with the fruit and place them in the slow cooker. Add the cold water, (to surround the apples), cover and cook on a low temperature for 7 to 8 hours.

Baklavas (Serves 6)

5 whole cloves
1 tsp ground cinnamon
1 cinnamon stick
2 tbsps clear honey
225g/1 1/2 cups of mixed nuts (chopped)
75g/1/3 cup of butter (unsalted)
12 sheets of filo pastry (all buttered)
170g/3/4 cup of dark brown sugar
150ml/2/3 cup of water

1. Preheat the oven to 190C/375F/Gas mark 5. Grease a Swiss roll tin with butter. Take 4 sheets of the filo pastry and layer the base of the tin.

2. Place the sugar, nuts and cinnamon in a bowl and mix together. Sprinkle half of the mixture over the pastry in the tin. Layer over the top with another 4 sheets of filo pastry and cover with the other half of the sugar/nuts mixture.

3. Layer the final 4 sheets of filo pastry over the top. Cut the edges, where needed, and cut the pastry into the required number of rectangles. Place in the oven and cook for 25-30 minutes, until lightly browned. Remove from the oven and allow to cool for a couple of minutes.

4. Place the remaining sugar in a saucepan with the clear honey, cloves and cinnamon stick. Add the water and bring to the boil. Reduce the heat and simmer for 8-10 minutes.

5. Pour the spiced mixture over the still-warm baklavas and leave to cool for 5-10 minutes.

Banana & Berry Delight with Nutmeg (Serves 4)
1 tsp nutmeg
2 large bananas (or 3 small)
175g/1 1/2 cups of frozen or fresh cranberries
60g/1/2 cup of oats
4 scoops of low-fat frozen yoghurt

1. Cut the bananas into 1/2 inch pieces. Mix all the ingredients together in a non-stick frying pan and cook on a medium heat, stirring occasionally. Once the cranberries begin to soften, remove from the heat and leave to cool for one minute.

2. Serve the mixture into bowls and finish off with a scoop of low-fat frozen yoghurt, if desired.

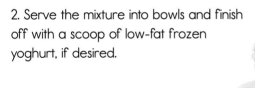

Cherry & Almond Spice Slices (Makes 24)

1/2 tsp ground nutmeg
2 tsps ground cinnamon
375g/1 2/3 cups of butter (softened)
395g/1 3/4 cups of glace cherries (washed, dried & chopped)
315g/2 3/4 cups of plain flour
200g/1 3/4 cups of self raising flour
340g/1 1/2 cups of caster sugar
100g ground rice
4 eggs (beaten)
2 tbsps Demerara sugar
2 tbsps slivered almond flakes

1. Preheat the oven to 180C/350F/Gas mark 4. Line two 28cm x 18cm baking tins with baking paper. Place the 200g of butter and 100g of caster sugar in a bowl and beat together well, until fluffy.

2. Sift the plain flour into a bowl and add the cinnamon and ground rice; gently fold together, making a soft dough. Divide equally and press into the bases of the baking tins.

3. Sprinkle the chopped cherries evenly over the surface of the dough. Place the remaining caster sugar and butter together and then fold in the self raising flour and eggs. Combine well. Spoon the mixture equally over the dough/cherries and level off the surface with the back of a spoon.

4. Sprinkle over with the almonds and Demerara sugar, followed by the nutmeg. Make sure that you do this as evenly as possible.

5. Place in the oven for 35-40 minutes, until lightly browned and firm to touch. Remove from the oven and leave to cool on a wire cooling rack. Once cooled, peel the baking paper away and cut into 12 slices, per baking tray

Cinnamon & Chilli Chocolate Fondue (Serves 10-12)

2 tsps ground cinnamon
1 tsp crushed chillies
450g milk or plain chocolate
400ml/1 3/4 cups of double cream
Grated zest of 1 orange
Selection of fruits for dipping

1. Place the chocolate, orange zest, crushed chillies and cinnamon in a bowl and set over a pan of simmering water. Once the chocolate has melted gradually stir in the cream. Combine well.

2. Pour the mixture into a fondue or serving bowl and serve with a selection of fruits around the outside.

Fruit & Rum Cake (Serves 6-8)

2 tsps ground ginger
2 tsps ground cinnamon
2 tsps ground nutmeg
220g/1 1/4 cups of pitted dates (chopped)
375g/2 1/2 cups of sultanas
345g/3 cups of self raising flour
170g/3/4 cups of dark brown sugar
225g/1 cup of butter (softened)
3 large eggs (beaten)
3 1/2 tbsps dark rum
3 tbsps black treacle

1. Preheat the oven to 150C/300F/Gas mark 2. Line a 20½ cm square cake tin with 2 layers of baking paper. Place the butter and sugar in a bowl and beat together until light and fluffy. Beat the eggs into the mixture, a little at a time, adding a tablespoon of flour each time.

2. Add any remaining flour and the ginger, cinnamon and nutmeg. Stir in the rum, dates and sultanas; mixing them in evenly. Spoon the mixture into the cake and make a slight hollow in the centre of the mixture, to allow it to rise sufficiently. Place in the oven and cook for 1½-2 hours, until the cake has risen and is firm to the touch.

Fruit & Spice Marmalade

1/4 tsp freshly ground nutmeg

1/2 tsp ground cinnamon

1/4 tsp ground ginger

2 1/2 lbs peaches (ripe, peeled & finely chopped)

1 orange (sliced into 1/4 inch wedges, with rind)

55ml/1/4 cup of lemon juice

75g powdered fruit pectin

900g/4 cups of granulated sugar

1. Place the lemon juice, orange wedges, peaches and fruit pectin in a saucepan and heat over a high temperature. Bring to the boil, stirring continuously.

2. Add the sugar and bring back to the boil. Boil on a high heat for 1½ minutes, stirring continuously. Take off the heat and remove any surface foam from the top of the mixture.

3. Stir in the ginger, nutmeg and cinnamon; combine well. Pour the mixture into clean jars and seal.

Fruit & Spice Squares (Makes 20-24)

Cake:

1 tsp nutmeg

1 tsp cinnamon

1 tsp allspice

2 eggs

75g/1/3 cup of light brown sugar

115g/1 cup of wholemeal flour

100g/1 cup of banana (mashed)

60g/1/2 cup of walnuts (chopped)

75g/1 1/2 cups of carrots (peeled & grated)

75g/1/3 cup of butter (melted)

1 tsp baking powder

Topping:

150ml/2/3 cup of whipping cream

115g quark

1. Preheat the oven to 190C/375F/Gas mark 5. Grease a 18cm x 28cm baking tray and line it with baking paper. Place the egg and sugar in a bowl and whisk together until think and creamy. Add the butter and whisk in.

2. Add the mashed banana, grated carrot, chopped walnuts and the spices and combine well. Sift the flour and baking powder into a bowl and gradually fold into the wet ingredients, until well mixed.

3. Transfer the mixture into the baking tin and spread evenly with a blunt knife or the back of a spoon. Place in the oven for 20 minutes, until firm to the touch.

4. Remove from the oven and leave to cool for 10 minutes. Turn out onto a wire cooling rack to cool completely. Place the quark and cream in a bowl and beat together, until creamy. Spread over the top of the cake base and cut into the desired number of squares.

Ginger & Spice Chutney (Makes 2-3 pints)
1/4 tsp whole cloves
1/4 tsp whole allspice
1 1/2 cinnamon sticks
1/2 cup of chopped crystallised ginger
340ml/1 1/2 cups of cider vinegar
450g/2 cups of granulated sugar
900g/4 cups of ripe pears (peeled & sliced)
115g/3/4 cup raisins
45g/1/4 cup green bell pepper (finely chopped)
1/4 tsp salt

1. Place the raisins, ginger, sugar, pears, cider vinegar, salt and chopped peppers in a saucepan. Add the cinnamon sticks. Tie the cloves and allspice inside a cheesecloth bag or cloth and add to the saucepan.

2. Cook over a gentle heat for 50-60 minutes, until the pears are tender and the mixture has thickened. Remove the cheesecloth and cinnamon sticks.

Ginger & Spice Chutney/continued

3. Transfer the liquid into warmed jars, (leaving a 1 inch gap at the top), and carefully run a spatula around the insides to release any trapped air bubbles.

4. Place the lids on the jars and immerse in a boiling water bath-canner for 8-10 minutes. Remove and leave to cool overnight. Store in a dry, cool place.

Spiced Chocolate Raisin Cookies (Makes 36)

1/2 tsp ground cinnamon
1/4 tsp ground nutmeg
Pinch of allspice
60g/1/2 cup of whole wheat flour
30g/1/4 cup of plain flour
100g chocolate raisins
1/4 tsp baking powder
1/2 tbsp molasses
110g/1/2 cup of butter (softened)
110g/1/2 cup of light brown sugar
1 egg (lightly beaten)
150g/1 1/2 cups of rolled oats
(not instant)

1. Place the plain flour, whole wheat flour, cinnamon, allspice, nutmeg and baking powder in a bowl and mix together.

2. Place the molasses, butter and brown sugar in a large bowl and beat with a hand-held electric blender. Beat for a few minutes, until the mixture becomes light and fluffy. Beat in the egg. Gradually add the flour and spice mixture, mixing in a little at a time.

3. Carefully fold in the chocolate raisins and rolled oats; combine well with a wooden spoon. Place the dough in the refrigerator for 45-60 minutes, until the dough is fairly firm.

4. Whilst the dough is firming, preheat the oven to 180C/350F/Gas mark 4 and line 4 baking trays with baking paper.

5. Remove the dough from the fridge and scoop put the dough, one per tablespoon. Roll each dough piece into a ball and gently flatten with the palm of the hand.

6. Place the cookies onto the baking trays, 1½ inches apart. Place in the oven for 16-18 minutes, until golden brown.

7. Remove from the oven and leave to cool for 6-8 minutes. Transfer the cookies to a wire cooling rack to cool completely.

Spiced Dessert Breadcrumbs
(Serves 1 Dessert Topping)
1/2 tsp cinnamon
100g/2 cups of fresh
Breadcrumbs
30g/1/8 cup of butter
1 tbsp sugar

1. Heat the butter in a frying pan and add the breadcrumbs. Cook for 2-3 minutes, stirring continuously until the butter has been absorbed.

2. Sprinkle over the sugar and cinnamon and mix in well. Continue to cook until golden brown.

3. Turn out onto paper kitchen roll to absorb any residual fat.

Serve as a topping for ice-cream, yoghurt, fruit or custards.

Spiced Fruit (Serves 4-6)

1 tsp ground nutmeg
1 tsp ground cinnamon
350g/1 3/4 cups of canned pineapple chunks (undrained)
700g/4 cups of canned pear slices (drained)
700g/4 cups of canned peach slices (drained)
110g/1/2 cup of maraschino cherries (drained)
425g canned mixed fruit salad
50g/1/4 cup of brown sugar
1 tbsp cornstarch
2 tbsps butter

1. This recipe should be cooked in a slow cooker, but if you do not have one, cook in a conventional oven on the lowest heat possible.

2. Place all of the ingredients in the slow cooker or casserole dish and mix together well.

3. Cover and cook for 4 to 6 hours. Serve in individual serving bowls with double cream.

Spiced Oats 'n' Apples (Serves 2)

Pinch of nutmeg
Pinch of cinnamon
2 diced apples
80g/1/3 cup of quick-cook rolled oats
335ml/1 1/2 cups of apple juice
335ml/1 1/2cups of water

1. Place the apples, juice, water and spices in a pan and mix well. Place over a medium to high heat and bring to the boil.

2. Stir in the oats thoroughly and cook for 1 minute. Remove from heat, cover and stand for 3 minutes before serving equally into 2 bowls.

Traditional Bread & Butter Pudding (Serves 4-6)

1 tsp cinnamon
1 tsp vanilla
100g/2 cups of bread (cubed)
110g/1/2 cup of brown sugar
75g/1/2 cup of raisins
2 eggs (lightly beaten)
500ml/2 1/4 cups of milk
1/4 tsp salt
110ml/1/2 cup of water

1. This recipe should be cooked in a slow cooker, but if you do not have one, cook in a conventional oven on the lowest heat possible. Place the eggs and milk in a large mixing bowl and whisk together. Add the bread, vanilla, sugar, raisins, cinnamon and salt and combine well.

2. Pour the mixture into a baking, or soufflé dish (one which will fit into your slow cooker). To keep the dish off the bottom of the slow cooker, use either a metal rack, or make a padded ring out of foil.

3. Add 1/2 cup of water to the slow cooker and place the baking/soufflé dish on top of the rack, or foil ring. Cover and cook for 1 1/2 to 2 1/2 hours, until the pudding is set.

Something sweet!

Tropical Spiced Fruit Salad (Serves 6-8)

10 cardamom pods

1 vanilla pod

2 cinnamon sticks

1 tsp arrowroot (mixed with 2 tsp water)

300ml/1 1/3 cups of orange juice

100g/1 cup of blueberries

3 kiwis (cubed)

1 mango (cubed)

415g/2 3/4 cups of melon (cubed)

2 passion fruits (flesh only)

2 tsps sugar

3-4 tbsps Grand Marnier

1. Place the Grand Marnier, orange juice, sugar, vanilla pod, cardamom pods and cinnamon sticks in a saucepan and bring to the boil. Reduce the heat and simmer on a low heat for 4-5 minutes.

2. Add the blended arrowroot to the saucepan and return to the boil, stir continuously until the mixture thickens. Leave to cool.

3. Remove the whole spices and stir in the fruit. Refrigerate for 1-2 hours before serving. Serve with crème fraiche or frozen yoghurt.

Drinks

Drinks

Apple Pie & Custard Smoothie (Serves 1)
1/4 tsp ground cinnamon
110ml/1/2 cup of apple juice (cold)
110ml/1/4 cup of ready-made-custard (cold)

1. Place the apple juice and custard in a food processor and blend together. Pour out into a large glass and sprinkle over the top with cinnamon.

Cardamom & Ginger Tea
8 cardamom pods
8 black peppercorns
1 cinnamon stick (large)
1 inch of root ginger (peeled & thinly sliced)
Drizzle of honey
Milk
560ml/2 1/2 cups of water

1. Place the cardamom pods, peppercorns, cinnamon, ginger and water in a saucepan and bring to the boil. Reduce the heat and simmer for 25-30 minutes.

2. Strain the liquid into cups and serve with a drizzle of honey and milk, according to taste.

Celery & Artichoke Pick-Up Juice with Mint (Serves 2)
4 celery sticks
190g/1 1/4 cup of celeriac
200g/1 1/2 cups of artichokes
Handful of fresh mint

1. Juice the vegetables and the mint, taking care to alternate the mint leaves with each of the vegetables, (to prevent clogging).

2. Pour the liquid into a food processor and add some ice cubes.

Chilli Juice with Coriander (Serves 2)
2 tbsps coriander leaves (finely chopped)
1 small chilli (deseeded)
400g/2 cups of pineapple chunks
4 carrots
Juice of 1 lime

1. Juice the chilli, carrots and pineapple and pour into 2 tall glasses, over ice cubes. Equally divide the lime juice and stir in, followed by an equal amount of coriander in each glass. Stir well and serve.

Cinnamon, Apple & Prune Smoothie (Serves 1)
1/4 tsp ground cinnamon
340ml/1 1/2 cups of apple juice
3 tbsps Greek yoghurt
60g/1/2 cup of pitted prunes (chopped)
Pinch of cinnamon (to sprinkle)

1. Place the prunes and cinnamon in a bowl and mix together. Pour in the apple juice, cover and refrigerate overnight.

2. The following day, place the apple/prune mixture and yoghurt in a food processor and blend until smooth.

3. Pour into a large glass and add ice cubes. Sprinkle the top with a little cinnamon and serve.

Cucumber & Mint Smoothie (Serves 2)
1 1/2 handfuls of fresh mint (chopped)
1 cucumber (peeled & deseeded)
500g/2 cups of natural yoghurt
1/4 tsp salt
4 mint leaves

1. Place the cucumber, mint, yoghurt and salt in a food processor and blend until smooth. Pour into 2 tall glasses, with ice cubes. Garnish the top with mint leaves, if desired.

Drinks

Mulled Apple Cider (Serves 4)

1/4 tsp nutmeg
1/4 tsp cardamom
1/4 tsp whole cloves
1 cinnamon stick
1 bay leaf
900ml/4 cups apple cider
Zest of 1 orange (peeled, not grated)
1/8 cup of light brown sugar
55ml/1/4 cup of rum or brandy

1. Place all of the ingredients, (except the rum or brandy), in a saucepan and mix together. Bring to the boil, reduce the heat and simmer for 25-30 minutes.

2. Strain the liquid into a large heat-resistant jug, discarding the spices and peel. Add the rum or brandy and stir. Serve immediately.

Red Tomato, Coriander & Tabasco Kicker! (Serves 2)

20g/1 oz coriander
2 small fennel bulbs
4 large tomatoes
20g/1 oz spring onions
Tabasco sauce
Black pepper

1. Juice the fennel, tomatoes, spring onions and coriander and pour into 2 tall glasses.

2. Sprinkle with black pepper and add a dash of Tabasco sauce to each. Serve immediately.

Drinks

91

Spicy, Hot Lemonade! (Makes 4-6)

1/8 tsp ground cloves
1/2 tbsp vanilla extract
110ml/1/2 cup of lemon juice
950ml/4 1/4 cups of water
225g/1 cup of sugar
225ml/1 cup of orange juice

1. Place all the ingredients into a large saucepan and bring to the boil. Reduce the heat and simmer for 1-2 minutes. Serve hot, or leave to cool and refrigerate.

Traditional Spiced Mulled Wine (Makes 24 glasses or 12 half-pint mugs)

2 bottles medium or full-bodied red wine
(Bulgarian Cabernet Sauvignon is ideal)
1.5 litres water
1 orange, studded with 10 cloves
2 oranges and 2 lemons, sliced
6 tbsps sugar or honey
5cm cinnamon stick
2 tsps finely grated fresh root ginger
2 tbsps fruit liqueur such as Cointreau, Grand Marnier or cherry brandy

1. Mix all the ingredients together in a slow cooker or a large saucepan. Heat very gently for about 20 minutes. Do not boil, or this will boil off the alcohol.

2. Stir gently to ensure that the sugar or honey has dissolved. Keep warm over a low heat and serve.

Index and
Conversions

index

Index

Index

The recipes contained in this book are passed on in good faith but the publisher cannot be held responsible for any adverse results. Please be aware that certain recipes may contain nuts. The recipes use both metric and imperial measurements, and the reader should not mix metric and imperial measurements. Spoon measurements are level, teaspoons are assumed to be 5ml, tablespoons 15ml. For other measurements, see chart below. Times given are for guidance only, as preparation techniques may vary and can lead to different cooking times.

Spoons to millilitres

1/2 teaspoon	2.5 ml	1 Tablespoon	15 ml
1 teaspoon	5 ml	2 Tablespoons	30 ml
1-1 1/2 teaspoons	7.5 ml	3 Tablespoons	45 ml
2 teaspoons	10 ml	4 Tablespoons	60 ml

Grams to ounces

10g	0.25oz	225g	8oz
15g	0.38oz	250g	9oz
25g	1oz	275g	10oz
50g	2oz	300g	11oz
75g	3oz	350g	12oz
110g	4oz	375g	13oz
150g	5oz	400g	14oz
175g	6oz	425g	15oz
200g	7oz	450g	16oz

Metric to cups

Description		
Flour etc	115g	1 cup
Clear honey etc	350g	1 cup
Liquids etc	225ml	1 cup

Liquid measures

5fl oz	/4 pint	150 ml
7.5fl oz		215 ml
10fl oz	1/2 pint	275 ml
15fl oz		425 ml
20fl oz	1 pint	570 ml
35fl oz		1 litre

Conversions

Oven Temperatures

Gas mark	°F	°C
1	275°F	140°C
2	300°F	150°C
3	325°F	170°C
4	350°F	180°C
5	375°F	190°C
6	400°F	200°C
7	425°F	220°C
8	450°F	230°C
9	475°F	240°C

Conversions